A

Math in Focus
Singapore Math
by Marshall Cavendish

Extra Practice

Author

Leong May Kuen

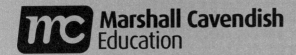
Marshall Cavendish
Education

COMMON CORE

US Distributor

 HOUGHTON MIFFLIN HARCOURT

© 2013 Marshall Cavendish International (Singapore) Private Limited

Published by Marshall Cavendish Education
An imprint of Marshall Cavendish International (Singapore) Private Limited
Times Centre, 1 New Industrial Road, Singapore 536196
Customer Service Hotline: (65) 6411 0820
E-mail: tmesales@sg.marshallcavendish.com
Website: www.marshallcavendish.com/education

Distributed by
Houghton Mifflin Harcourt
222 Berkeley Street
Boston, MA 02116
Tel: 617-351-5000
Website: www.hmheducation.com/mathinfocus

Cover: © Mike Hill/Getty Images

First published 2013

Math in Focus® Extra Practice Course 3A
ISBN 978-0-547-57907-8

Printed in United States of America

2 3 4 5 6 7 8   1401   17 16 15 14 13 12
4500358143   A B C D E

Contents

Math in Focus®
Singapore Math
by Marshall Cavendish

Introducing Math in Focus® Extra Practice

Extra Practice was written to complement **Math in Focus®: Singapore Math by Marshall Cavendish**. It offers further practice for on-level students and is very similar to the Practice exercises in the Student Books.

Practice to Reinforce and Challenge

Extra Practice provides ample questions to reinforce all concepts taught, and includes challenging questions in the Brain@Work pages. These challenging questions provide extra non-routine problem-solving opportunities, strengthening abstract reasoning powers that include the use of mathematical structures, repeated patterns, models, and tools.

Using the Cumulative Practice

Extra Practice also provides Cumulative Practices that allow students to consolidate learning from several chapters. They can be used to prepare for Benchmark Tests or as another source of good problems for class discussion.

Using the Extra Practice

Extra Practice is an excellent option for homework, or it may be used in class or after school. It is intended for students who simply need more practice to become confident, secure mathematics students who are aiming for excellence.

 Extra Practice is also available online and on the Teacher One Stop CD-ROM.

CHAPTER

 Exponents

Lesson 1.1   Exponential Notation

Identify the base and the exponent in each expression.

1. 5^2

2. 8^4

3. -3^8

4. $\left(\dfrac{3}{7}\right)^9$

5. $(-2)^4$

6. 1.7^8

Tell whether each statement is correct. If it is incorrect, state the reason.

7. $-8^3 = -8 \cdot -8 \cdot -8$

8. $17^4 = 17 \cdot 17 \cdot 17 \cdot 17$

Write in exponential notation.

9. $6.7 \cdot 6.7 \cdot 6.7 \cdot 6.7$

10. $\dfrac{2}{9} \cdot \dfrac{2}{9} \cdot \dfrac{2}{9}$

11. $27 \cdot 27 \cdot 27 \cdot 27$

12. $(-9) \cdot (-9) \cdot (-9)$

13. $ab \cdot ab \cdot ab \cdot ab$

14. $w \cdot w \cdot w \cdot w \cdot w \cdot w$

Name: _____   Date: _____

Expand and evaluate each expression.

15. -8.8^3

16. 3^2

17. 5^3

18. $\left(\dfrac{4}{9}\right)^3$

Write the prime factorization of each number in exponential notation.

19. 1,568

20. 18,225

21. 81

Order the following expressions from least to greatest.

22. -8^4, 8^4, and -4^8

23. $(-6)^2$, $(-2)^6$, -2^6

Solve. Show your work.

24. The mass of Mars is approximately 100,000,000,000,000,000,000,000 kilograms, and that of Neptune is about 100,000,000,000,000,000,000,000,000 kilograms. Write each mass as 10 raised to a power.

Solve. Show your work.

25. Bacteria are single-celled organisms that can divide and multiply very rapidly when moisture and nutrients are present. The diagram shows the cell division of one bacterium.

0 min

20 min

40 min

Find the number of bacteria present after 80 minutes if there were two bacteria at 0 minutes. Give your answer in exponential notation.

26. Kelly folded a large piece of square paper along its diagonal. She noticed that two triangles were formed. Then she made a second fold and four triangles were formed. The following table shows the result of her folds of the square paper.

Number of Folds	Number of Triangles Formed on Square Paper
1	2
2	4
3	8

How many folds must Kelly make to obtain 128 triangles on the square paper?

Lesson 1.2   The Product and Quotient of Powers

Simplify each expression. Write your answer in exponential notation.

1. $5^8 \cdot 5^2$

2. $3.2^4 \cdot 3.2^5$

3. $\left(\dfrac{7}{9}\right)^2 \cdot \left(\dfrac{7}{9}\right)^6$

4. $(-12)^8 \cdot (-12)$

5. $q^4 \cdot q^3$

6. $m^9 \div m^5$

7. $6xy^2 \cdot 3x^7y^2$

8. $4.5a^3\,b^7 \cdot 2a^6\,b$

9. $(-7)^9 \div (-7)^2$

10. $\left(\dfrac{3}{4}\right)^8 \div \left(\dfrac{3}{4}\right)^5$

Name: _____   Date: _____

Simplify each expression. Write your answer in exponential notation.

11. $b^5c^8 \div b^3c^2$

12. $72x^9y^7 \div 8x^3y^5$

13. $\dfrac{8^9 \cdot 8^2 \cdot 8^6}{8^4 \cdot 8^2 \cdot 8^3}$

14. $\dfrac{\left(\frac{2}{3}\right)^7 \cdot \left(\frac{2}{3}\right)^3 \cdot \left(\frac{2}{3}\right)^9}{\left(\frac{2}{3}\right)^2 \cdot \left(\frac{2}{3}\right)^2 \cdot \left(\frac{2}{3}\right)^4}$

15. $\dfrac{y^3 \cdot y^8 \cdot y^6}{y^4 \cdot y^2 \cdot y^2}$

16. $\dfrac{5a^5 \cdot 7b^4 \cdot 2b^3}{b^5 \cdot 5b^2 \cdot 2a^4}$

Solve. Show your work.

17. The side length of cube A is 100,000 millimeters. The side length of cube B is 10^8 millimeters.

   a) Express the volume in cube A in cubic millimeters, using exponential notation.

   b) How many times greater is the volume of cube B than that of cube A?

18. A rectangular container has length 15p meters, width 12p meters, and height 6p meters. How many cubes each of length 2p meters can be packed into the rectangular container?

Name: _____ Date: _____

Lesson 1.3   The Power of a Power

Simplify each expression. Write your answer in exponential notation.

1. $(6^5)^3$

2. $(9^6)^4$

3. $(34^8)^2$

4. $(18^6)^7$

5. $(p^5)^4$

2. $\left[\left(\dfrac{6}{7}\right)^6\right]^3$

7. $[(4b)^4]^4$

8. $[(28x)^7]^2$

9. $[(-22)^5]^7$

10. $[(-2q)^4]^2$

Simplify each expression. Write your answer in exponential notation.

11. $(2^5 \cdot 2^3)^2$

12. $(q^7 \cdot q)^4$

13. $\left[\left(\dfrac{5}{6}\right)^3 \cdot \left(\dfrac{5}{6}\right)^2\right]^3$

14. $\left[\left(-\dfrac{9}{10}\right)^4 \cdot \left(-\dfrac{9}{10}\right)^8\right]^2$

Simplify each expression. Write your answer in exponential notation.

15. $(2^3 \cdot 2^6)^4 \div 2^8$

16. $(11^6 \cdot 11^6)^2 \div 11^9$

17. $(q^7 \cdot q^3)^4 \div q^5$

18. $(y^9 \cdot y)^3 \div y^{13}$

19. $\dfrac{(3^3 \cdot 3^5)^4}{(3^8)^2}$

20. $\dfrac{(w^9 \cdot w^5)^4}{(w^2)^5}$

21. $(u^3 \cdot u^6)^4 \div 8u^2$

22. $(p^2 \cdot p^5)^9 \div 7p^3$

23. $\dfrac{\left(\dfrac{3}{7}\right)^5 \cdot \left(\dfrac{9}{7}\right)^2}{\left(\dfrac{3^4}{7^3}\right)^2}$

24. $\dfrac{\left(\dfrac{y}{5}\right)^2 \cdot \left(\dfrac{y^3}{5}\right)^5}{\left(\dfrac{y^2}{5}\right)^6}$

Lesson 1.4   The Power of a Product and the Power of a Quotient

Simplify each expression. Write your answer in exponential notation.

1. $7^3 \cdot 4^3$

2. $8.3^5 \cdot 1.2^5$

3. $\left(\dfrac{3}{7}\right)^4 \cdot \left(\dfrac{1}{2}\right)^4$

4. $\left(-\dfrac{4}{5}\right)^6 \cdot \left(-\dfrac{2}{3}\right)^6$

5. $p^8 \cdot w^8$

6. $(5b)^2 \cdot (3c)^2$

7. $(6x)^3 \cdot (1.2y)^3$

8. $w^9 \div v^9$

9. $(5c)^5 \div (2b)^5$

10. $(8.2y)^4 \div (2x)^4$

Simplify each expression. Write your answer in exponential notation.

11. $21^6 \div 3^6$

12. $1.8^3 \div 0.3^3$

13. $9.6^5 \div 3^5$

14. $12^9 \div 21^9$

15. $(-20)^2 \div (-5)^2$

16. $(p^6 q^2)^3$

17. $\left(\dfrac{36b^3}{9a^5} \right)^3$

18. $\dfrac{25^2 \cdot 25^6}{5^4 \cdot 5}$

19. $\dfrac{8^7 \cdot 8^4 \cdot 2^3}{16^3}$

20. $\dfrac{(9^3)^4 \cdot 6^{12}}{27^{12}}$

21. $\dfrac{3^6 \cdot (16^3)^2}{12^6}$

22. $\dfrac{18^8}{6^3 \cdot 3^4 \cdot 6^5}$

Lesson 1.5   Zero and Negative Exponents

Simplify each expression and evaluate where applicable.

1. $9^4 \cdot 9^0$

2. $11^3 \cdot (-11)^0$

3. $\left(\dfrac{6}{7}\right)^8 \cdot \left(\dfrac{6}{7}\right)^0$

4. $9^2 \cdot 10^3 + 5^3 \cdot 10^2 + 2^6 \cdot 10^0$

5. $4.7 \cdot 10^3 + 6 \cdot 10^2 + 7 \cdot 10^0$

6. $\dfrac{5^3 \cdot 5^7}{5^{10}}$

7. $(4^{-2})^0 \cdot 7^2$

8. $\dfrac{(8^{-4})^{-2} \cdot 7^8}{56^8}$

Simplify each expression. Write your answer using a negative exponent.

9. $6^{-8} \cdot 6^3$

10. $\dfrac{(-9)^{-4}}{(-9)^4}$

11. $\dfrac{5}{6} \div \left[\left(\dfrac{5}{6}\right)^7 \cdot \left(\dfrac{5}{6}\right)^0\right]$

12. $\left(\dfrac{3}{8}\right)^{-5} \cdot \left(\dfrac{3}{8}\right)^{-2} \div \left(\dfrac{3}{8}\right)^{-1}$

13. $\dfrac{y^0}{y^4 \cdot y^3}$

14. $\dfrac{7p^{-6} \cdot 6p^{-3}}{3p^{-5}}$

Name: _____   Date: _____

Simplify each expression. Write your answer using a positive exponent.

15. $4.1^0 \div 3.6^5$

16. $9.6^{-4} \div 3.2^{-4}$

17. $\dfrac{(-6)^{-8}}{(-6)^3}$

18. $\left(\dfrac{4}{9}\right)^{-7} \cdot \left(\dfrac{4}{9}\right)^{-1} \div \left(\dfrac{4}{9}\right)^{-5}$

19. $\dfrac{5h^{-2} \cdot 7h^{-4}}{25h^{-9}}$

20. $\dfrac{b^{16} \cdot b^{-5}}{b^{-7}}$

Evaluate each numeric expression.

21. $\dfrac{4^{-3} \cdot 4^0}{9^4 \cdot 9^{-7}}$

22. $\dfrac{(5^{-2})^4 \cdot 16^{-8}}{40^{-8}}$

23. $\dfrac{6^0}{3^{-3} \cdot 2^{-3}}$

24. $\dfrac{(5^3)^{-4}}{10^{-8} \cdot (-2)^5}$

Simplify each algebraic expression.

25. $\left(\dfrac{8v^6}{-64w^0}\right)^{-1}$

26. $\dfrac{28x^4y^7}{4x^6y^{-1}}$

Lesson 1.6   Real-World Problems: Squares and Cubes

Find the two square roots of each number. Round your answer to the nearest tenth if necessary.

1. 81

2. 36

3. 97

4. 140

Find the cube root of each number. Round your answer to the nearest tenth if necessary.

5. 216

6. 343

7. 682

8. $\dfrac{27}{512}$

Solve each equation involving a variable that is squared.

9. $h^2 = 50.41$

10. $d^2 = \dfrac{49}{81}$

11. $a^2 = 144$

12. $m^2 = 295$

Name: _____   Date: _____

 Solve each equation involving a variable that is cubed. Write fractions in simplest form, and round decimal answers to the nearest tenth.

13. $s^3 = 50.653$

14. $s^3 = \dfrac{27}{343}$

15. $s^3 = 2,744$

16. $s^3 = 3,800$

 Solve. Show your work. Round to the nearest tenth.

17. The surface area of a spherical lampshade is 57.76π square inches. What is the radius of the lampshade?

18. A spherical solid of volume 123,456 cubic meters is melted and recast into a solid cube. What is the side length of the cube?

19. A square box can store 2,940 cylindrical cans. Each cylindrical can occupies a square base area of 15 square centimeters. What is the length of the box?

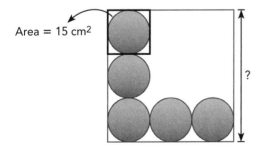

Area = 15 cm²

?

CHAPTER

1 Brain @ Work

State whether each of the following is true or false? Explain your answers.

1. $x^4 + x^7 = x^{11}$

2. $8y^5 \div 4y = 4y^4$

Solve. Show your work.

3. The formula $T_n = ar^{n-1}$ can be used to find the nth term of a sequence of numbers, where a is the first term in the sequence and r is the common ratio.

For example, in the sequence 10, 40, 160, 640, ..., $a = 10$, and
$r = \dfrac{40}{10} = \dfrac{160}{40} = \dfrac{640}{160} = 4$.

In the given sequence, use the formula to find the product of the 10th and 13th terms and when the 10th term is divided by the 13th term. Express your answers in exponential notation.

$$\frac{1}{2}, 1, 2, 4, 8, 16, \ldots$$

CHAPTER

2 Scientific Notation

Lesson 2.1   Understanding Scientific Notation

Tell whether each number is written correctly in scientific notation. If incorrectly written, state the reason.

1. $9 \cdot 10^{15}$

2. $21.5 \cdot 10^{-5}$

3. $7.25 \cdot 10^{23}$

4. $0.8 \cdot 10^{7}$

Write each number in scientific notation.

5. 6,238

6. 3,700,000,000

7. 0.00000000000083

8. 0.0028

Write each number in standard form.

9. $6.05 \cdot 10^{1}$

10. $8.4 \cdot 10^{5}$

11. $3.82 \cdot 10^{-4}$

12. $9.8 \cdot 10^{-7}$

Identify the greater number in each pair of numbers. Justify your reasoning.

13. $5.8 \cdot 10^{5}$ and $8.5 \cdot 10^{3}$

14. $9.9 \cdot 10^{10}$ and $9.6 \cdot 10^{11}$

15. $4.8 \cdot 10^{-7}$ and $8.8 \cdot 10^{-7}$

16. $1.25 \cdot 10^{-3}$ and $1.28 \cdot 10^{-5}$

Name: _____   Date: _____

Solve. Show your work.

17. Dylan came across the following fun facts about the human body while searching the internet. Complete the table by writing each figure in scientfic notation.

Fun Facts	Fun Figures in Standard Form	Fun Figures in Scientific Notation
Number of cells in a human body	12,000,000,000,000	
The diameter of a red blood cell (m)	0.0000084	
Average number of times the human eye blinks	4,200,000	
Number of hairs on a human scalp	100,000	
The width of a human hair (cm)	0.00108	
Average number of times a human heart beats in its lifetime	3,000 million	

18. Airborne particles are solids suspended in the air. The table shows the sizes of some airborne particles.

Airborne Particles	Particle Diameter (m)	Particle Diameter in Scientific Notation (m)
Saw dust	0.000085	
Talcum dust	0.00000024	
Carbon black dust	0.0000007	
Cement dust	0.000018	

Note: The size of contaminants and particles are usually described in microns, a metric unit of measure, where one micron is one-millionth of a meter.

a) Complete the table by writing each particle diameter in scientific notation.

b) If a human eye can see particles to approximately $4 \cdot 10^{-5}$ meter, which airborne particles listed in the table are visible to humans?

Name: _____   Date: _____

Solve. Show your work.

19. At a science fair, Julia came across the following data:
    - The average human eye blink takes $3.5 \cdot 10^5$ microseconds.
    - A camera flash illuminates for 1,000 microseconds.
    - The shutter speed of a standard camera is $4 \cdot 10^3$ microseconds.

    Note: A microsecond is an SI unit of time equal to one millionth (10^{-6}) of a second. Its symbol is μs.

    a) Which action listed takes the least amount of time, in microseconds, to complete?
       Write your answer in scientific notation.

    b) Which action listed takes the greatest amount of time, in microseconds, to complete?
       Write your answer in scientific notation.

20. The table shows the speed of two mediums in air.

Medium	Speed (m/s)	Speed in Scientific Notation (m/s)
Light	300 million	
Sound	330	

    a) Complete the table by writing the speed of each medium in scientific notation.

    b) Which is most likely to occur first, a person seeing a flash of lightning or a person hearing the sound of thunder?

Lesson 2.2   Adding and Subtracting in Scientific Notation

Solve. Show your work. Round the coefficient to the nearest tenth.

1. $7.8 \cdot 10^5 + 3.9 \cdot 10^6$

2. $11.4 \cdot 10^{-3} - 9.8 \cdot 10^{-3}$

3. $5.6 \cdot 10^{-2} + 8.6 \cdot 10^{-1}$

4. $6.5 \cdot 10^7 - 2.8 \cdot 10^6$

Use the table to answer questions 5 to 7. Round the coefficient to the nearest tenth.

The table shows the mass, in grams, of a grain of a substance.

Substances	Mass (g)
A grain of salt	$5.85 \cdot 10^{-5}$
A grain of sand	$6 \cdot 10^{-4}$
A grain of rice	$2 \cdot 10^{-2}$
A grain of sugar	$6.5 \cdot 10^{-2}$

5. Find the total mass in each combination.

a) a grain of salt and a grain of sand

b) a grain of rice and a grain of sugar

6. What is the difference in mass between a grain of salt and a grain of sand?

7. How much heavier/lighter is a grain of rice as compared to a grain of salt?

Name: _____   Date: _____

Solve. Show your work.

8. The driving distance between Phoenix and Los Angeles is 599 kilometers.
   The driving distance between Phoenix and Chicago is approximately
   $2.3 \cdot 10^3$ kilometers.

   a)   Which city is nearer to Phoenix, Los Angeles or Chicago?

   b)   If Bradley traveled from Phoenix to Los Angeles and Andy traveled
           from Phoenix to Chicago, what is the difference in the distance traveled?
           Write your answer in scientific notation and round the coefficient to the
           nearest tenth.

9. The diagram show a small ant and a large ant.

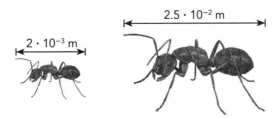

$$2.5 \cdot 10^{-2} \text{ m}$$

$$2 \cdot 10^{-3} \text{ m}$$

   The length of a small ant is $2 \cdot 10^{-3}$ meter and the length of a large ant is
   $2.5 \cdot 10^{-2}$ meter.

   a)   Find the difference in length, in millimeters, of the two ants. Write your
           answer in scientific notation.

   b)   If there is a trail of 2 small ants and 1 large ant in a straight line, find the
           total length of the trail.

Name: _____ Date: _____

Use the table to answer questions 10 to 13.

The table shows the number of public drinking water systems and the population served in three different cities in a particular year.

City	Number of Drinking Water Systems	Population Served
A	52,873	300,200,000
B	19,400	$6.4 \cdot 10^6$
C	87,672	13,100,000

10. Arrange the population served in each of the three cities in descending order.

11. Write the number of drinking water systems in each city in scientific notation by rounding the coefficient to the nearest tenth.

12. What is the difference in the population served in city A and city C? Write your answer in scientific notation.

13. Find the total population served in the three cities. Leave your answer in scientific notation and round the coefficient to the nearest tenth.

Name: _____   Date: _____

Lesson 2.3   Multiplying and Dividing in Scientific Notation

Evaluate each expression in scientific notation, and round the coefficient to the nearest tenth.

1. $8.5 \cdot 10^{-2} \cdot 9.52 \cdot 10^{7}$

2. $3.8 \cdot 10^{3} \div 4.86 \cdot 10^{-2}$

3. $6.2 \cdot 10^{5} \cdot 4.7 \cdot 10^{-8}$

4. $6.8 \cdot 10^{10} \div 2.3 \cdot 10^{-4}$

The table shows the approximate lengths, in miles, of some rivers in the United States. Use the information to answer questions 5 to 7. Round your answers to the nearest tenth.

Name of River	Length of River (mi)
Colorado River (Texas)	$8.94 \cdot 10^{2}$
Rio Grande	$1.885 \cdot 10^{3}$
Mississippi River	$3.860 \cdot 10^{3}$

5. About how many times as great as the length of Colorado River is the Mississippi River?

6. About how many times as great as the length of Colorado River is the Rio Grande?

7. About how many times as great as the length of the Rio Grande is the Mississippi River?

Name: _____ Date: _____

Solve. Show your work.

8. A certain type of bacteria can move at a speed of 220 micrometers per second.

    a) What is the distance, in meters, moved by the bacteria after 12 hours? Write your answer in scientific notation.

    b) Another type of bacteria moves $8 \cdot 10^{-7}$ meter per second. How far does this bacteria move in $5.45 \cdot 10^9$ seconds? Write your answer, in micrometers, using scientific notation.

9. The diagram shows a cube with sides of length 8 meters. A smaller cube with sides of length 3.5 meters has been cut out of the larger cube.

    a) Find the volume, in cubic centimeters, of the large cube before the small cube is cut out. Write your answer in scientific notation.

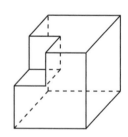

    b) Find the volume of the solid after the small cube is removed. Write your answer in scientific notation. Round the coefficient to the nearest tenth.

Name: _____   Date: _____

Solve. Show your work.

10. The table shows some models of LCD televisions and their native pixel resolution.

Model	Native Pixel Resolution
A	$1{,}280 \cdot 720$
B	$1{,}024 \cdot 768$
C	$1{,}366 \cdot 768$
D	$1{,}920 \cdot 1{,}080$

a) Express the given resolution of each model in the appropriate unit in prefix form to the nearest tenth.

b) All flat screen LCD televisions must have a resolution of at least one megapixel. Determine which models are not a flat screen LCD television.

11. The central processing unit (CPU) in a computer executes the computer instructions necessary to perform the designated task. 1.5 gigahertz means that the CPU is running at $1.5 \cdot 10^9$ hertz (or cycles per second).

a) Calculate how long the CPU takes to run one cycle. Express your answer in nanoseconds. Round the coefficient to the nearest hundredth.

b) If a computer has a processing speed of 1,700 million instructions per second, find the average number of cycles per instruction. Write your answer to the nearest unit.

Name: _____   Date: _____

Solve. Show your work.

12. The approximate diameter of a SARS virus is between $6 \cdot 10^{-8}$ meter and $2.2 \cdot 10^{-7}$ meter.

    a) Express the range of this diameter in prefix form using nanometers.

    b) A virus of diameter 48 nanometers has just been detected in a small community. Use the diameter to predict if this newly detected virus is a SARS virus?

13. The distance between town A and town B is 10 megameters while that between town A and town C is 100 kilometers. Is town B or town C nearer to town A?

14. A microscopic view of two organisms, P and Q, revealed their lengths as 25 nanometers and 2,500 picometers, respectively. Which organism has the greater length?

15. About 20,000 steel barrels were used for oil transport and storage. If each standard barrel has a diameter of 22.5 inches and 33.5 inches in height, how much oil is there altogether in the 20,000 steel barrels? Use 3.14 as an approximation for π. Write your answer in scientific notation and round the coefficient to the nearest tenth.

Name: _____   Date: _____

1. How many billions are there in a trillion?

2. A certain car manufacturer claims that their cars are installed with a device that prevents cars from being stolen. The key to a car has a unique code that only matches the one programmed in the car. There are altogether 72,000 trillion possible codes. Write this figure in scientific notation.

3. On a website, Max read that the radius of the Earth is approximately 6,300,000 meters and that the mass of the Earth is approximately $5.98 \cdot 10^{24}$ kilograms. Use this information to find an approximate value for the density of the Earth.

4. Without using a calculator, evaluate the following.

$$\sqrt{\frac{1.2 \cdot 10^{9} \cdot 4.5 \cdot 10^{-4}}{2 \cdot 10^{-2} \cdot 4.8 \cdot 10^{11}}}$$

Cumulative Practice
for Chapters 1 to 2

Write the prime factorization of each number in exponential notation.

1. 30,375

2. 29,400

Simplify each expression. Write your answer in exponential notation.

3. $\dfrac{\left[\left(\dfrac{3}{7}\right)^2 \cdot \left(\dfrac{3}{7}\right)^3\right]^3}{\left[\left(\dfrac{3}{7}\right)^2\right]^3}$

4. $(m^5 \cdot m^7)^4 \div (3m^2)^3$

Name: _____ Date: _____

Simplify each expression. Write your answer in positive exponential notation.

5. $\dfrac{7^4 \cdot 13^4}{(8^0)^4}$

6. $\dfrac{4^5 \cdot (-5^5) \cdot 5^0}{2^{-5}}$

7. $\left[16^3 \cdot 4^3\right]^4 \div 4^{12}$

8. $(81^6 \div 81^3) \cdot \dfrac{(6^0)^3}{3^3 \cdot 9^3}$

9. $12^{-3} \cdot \dfrac{5^0 \cdot 12^{-2}}{4^{-5}}$

10. $8^{-5} \cdot (6^0)^{-5} \cdot \left(\dfrac{1}{2}\right)^{-5} \div 3^{-5}$

Evaluate the square roots of each number. Write your answer to the nearest tenth if necessary.

11. 529

12. 1,056.2

Evaluate the cube root of each number. Write your answer to the nearest tenth if necessary.

13. $\dfrac{64}{343}$

14. -734.2

Evaluate each expression and write your answer in scientific notation. Identify the greater number.

15. $2.28 \cdot 10^{12} + 2.69 \cdot 10^{12}$ and $8.63 \cdot 10^{12} - 4.09 \cdot 10^{12}$

16. $7.4 \cdot 10^{-4} - 6.5 \cdot 10^{-5}$ and $3.6 \cdot 10^{-5} - 7.6 \cdot 10^{-6}$

Name: _____   Date: _____

Evaluate each expression and write your answer in scientific notation. Identify the greater number.

17. $4.8 \cdot 10^8 \cdot 5 \cdot 10^8$ and $7.3 \cdot 10^{-6} \cdot 4 \cdot 10^{-3}$

18. $8.4 \cdot 10^4 \div 7 \cdot 10^6$ and $7.5 \cdot 10^{-6} \div 1.5 \cdot 10^{-6}$

Write each of the following in the appropriate unit in prefix form.

19. 0.000000043 meter

20. 0.000093 second

21. 42,000,000,000 hertz

22. 69,000 bytes

Name: _____ Date: _____ Course 3A

Solve. Show your work.

23. The Great Pyramid of Khufu in Egypt is one of the Seven Wonders of the Ancient World. It is built on a square base with an approximate area of 53,065.73 square meters. What is the approximate side length of the square base? Round your answer to the nearest tenth.

24. The volume of the Moon is approximately $2.1958 \cdot 10^{10}$ cubic kilometers. Find the radius of the Moon, in kilometers, in scientific notation. Round the coefficient to the nearest tenth. Use 3.14 as an approximation for π.

25. The weight of an empty box is 56.7 grams. If there are 940 feathers with unit weight of 0.000567 kilogram in the box, find the total weight, in kilogram, of the box with 940 feathers inside. Write your answer in scientific notation. Round the coefficient to the nearest tenth.

11. $\dfrac{2(2x + 1)}{5} - \dfrac{x + 2}{3} = \dfrac{1}{5}$

12. $\dfrac{x + 3}{2} - \dfrac{11 - x}{5} = 1 + \dfrac{3x - 1}{20}$

Express each decimal as a fraction. Show your work.

13. $0.\overline{4}$

14. $0.0\overline{3}$

15. $0.1\overline{5}$

16. $0.2\overline{5}$

17. $0.41\overline{6}$

18. $0.3\overline{18}$

Solve each problem algebraically. Show your work.

19. Mabel paid $2.95 for a granola bar with dimes and quarters. She used 5 fewer quarters than dimes. How many dimes and quarters did she use to pay for the granola bar?

Solve each problem algebraically. Show your work.

20. Mrs. Willy bought $3\frac{1}{2}$ pounds of ground turkey and $2\frac{1}{2}$ pounds of white fish.

The white fish is $4.60 per pound cheaper than the ground turkey. If she paid a total of $51.50, what is the price per pound she paid for the ground turkey and the price per pound for the white fish?

21. Sylvia is carrying two bags of potatoes, bag A and bag B. The weight of bag B is 3 pounds more than twice the weight of bag A. The total weight of both bags of potatoes is 27 pounds. Find the weight of each bag of potatoes.

22. Gary is x years old today. Two years ago, his grandfather was 3 times older than Gary at that time.

a) The age difference of Gary and his grandfather is 48 years. Write a linear equation to represent this age difference.

b) Find Gary's grandfather's age today.

Name: _____   Date: _____

Solve each problem algebraically. Show your work.

23. There are 40 students in a class. The teacher gave each female student 5 counters and each male student 3 counters. After the distribution of the counters, the teacher realized that the female students had 128 more counters than the male student.

    a) Write and solve a linear equation to find the number of female students in the class.

24. Harry has 3 bamboo poles of different lengths. The total combined length of the three poles when placed end-to-end is $47\frac{1}{2}$ inches long. Pole B is $1\frac{3}{4}$ times as long as pole A and pole C is $2\frac{1}{2}$ inches longer than pole A.

    a) Write a linear equation for the total combined length of the 3 poles.

    b) Find the length of pole C.

Lesson 3.2   Identifying the Number of Solutions
to a Linear Equation

Tell whether each equation has one solution, no solution, or an infinite number of solutions. Justify your answer.

1. $\frac{4}{5}x + 18 = -2(3 + 2x)$

2. $7 + 2(x - 6) = -3 + 2(x - 1)$

3. $2\left(4 - \frac{1}{3}x\right) = x + 3(x - 2)$

4. $\frac{2}{5}(1 - 5x) = -\frac{1}{2}(4x + 3)$

5. $5(5 - 2x) - 6(2 - x) = 7(1 - x)$

6. $0.5(3x + 5) - 0.1(12x - 5) = 3(1 + 0.1x)$

7. $4(2 - x) + 2(1 - 5x) = 5(2 - 3x) + x$

8. $3\left(\frac{2}{9}x - 1\right) = 1 - \frac{2}{3}(x + 1) + \frac{4}{3}x$

9. $2(x + 5) - 2 = 1.5(10 - x)$

10. $2(x - 3) + \frac{1}{2}(7 + 2x) = \frac{1}{2} + 3(x - 1)$

Name: _____   Date: _____

Solve. Show your work.

11. The diagram shows 3 three-legged stools of different heights.

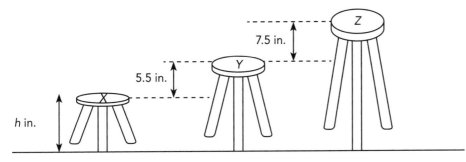

a) Write algebraic expressions for the heights hof stool Y and Z.

b) If twice the height of stool Z is equal to the sum of the height of stool X and Z, can you solve for the height of stool X? Explain.

12. In triangle ABC, AB is $6\left(3 - \frac{1}{4}x\right)$ centimeters and AC is $\left(\frac{3}{4}x + 5 - 2\frac{1}{4}x\right)$ centimeters. With these dimensions, can you conclude that the triangle is an isosceles triangle? Explain.

Lesson 3.3   Understanding Linear Equations with Two Variables

Write a linear equation for the relationship between the following quantities.

1. kilometers, k, and meters, m

2. pounds, l, and ounces, u

3. days, d, and hours, h

4. megabytes, m, and bytes, b

Find the value of y when $x = -3$

5. $4 - 2x = 8 + y$

6. $y = \dfrac{5}{4}(x + 7)$

7. $3(y - 5) = 5x + 3$

8. $7(x - 3) = 6y$

Find the value of x when $y = 5$

9. $3(x - 3) = 2y$

10. $\dfrac{5x - 3}{2} = 2(y + 3)$

11. $3x + 2y = 0.2(2y + 1)$

12. $7y - 4x = 51$

Name: _____   Date: _____

Create a table of *x* and *y* values for each of the following equations.
Use integer values of *x* from 2 to 4.

13. $y = \frac{1}{3}(9x - 18)$

14. $3x - 4 = \frac{1}{5}(y - 5)$

15. $-7y = 4x - 3$

16. $\frac{1}{4}(6x + 1) = \frac{1}{2}(y + 2)$

Complete the table of *x* and *y* values for each of the following equations.

17. $y = 4(2x + 1)$

x	1	2	3
y			

18. $x + \frac{y}{3} = 2$

x			3
y	9	3	

19. $4(y - 3x) = \dfrac{4}{5}$

x		1	2
y	$\dfrac{1}{5}$		

20. $3x = 5(y - 7)$

x			
y	−5	10	25

Solve. Show your work.

21. A new bakery shop sells rolls for $2 each. Before noon each day, if a customer buys 2 rolls or more, they receive a discount of $1. The table shows the cost, C in dollars, in terms of rolls purchased before noon.

Cost (C dollars)	3	5	7	9	11	13
Number of buns (n)	2	3	4	5	6	7

a) Write a linear equation for the cost, C, in terms of the number of buns, n, purchased before noon.

b) Find the cost of the 30 rolls that Mrs Carmen purchased before noon today.

Name: _____   Date: _____

Solve. Show your work.

22. A tank initially contains 50 liters of water. A tap adds water to the tank at a rate of 2 liters per minute.

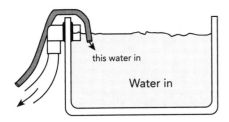

this water in

Water in

a) Write a linear equation for the amount of water in the tank, *W*, liters in terms of, *t*, minutes.

b) Use the equation in **a)** to complete the table of values below.

Time (*t* minutes)	20			80
Amount of Water in Tank (*W* liters)		130	170	210

c) How much water is in the tank after 5 hours?

d) The tank can hold 1,000 liters of water when filled completely. How long will it take to completely fill the tank? Write your answers in hours and minutes.

23. Joel has $40 in his piggy bank. He plans to add $7.50 a week when he starts his summer vacation job.

    a)   Write a linear equation for the amount in his bank, A dollars, in terms of time worked, t weeks.

    b)   Create a table of t and A values for the linear equation. Use $t = 4$, 6, and 8.

    c)   Find the number of weeks that Joel will have to save to buy a $175 season pass to a golf club.

24. Annabel sells sunscreen from a beach kiosk station. Each week, she receives $90 plus $0.25 for each tube of sunscreen that she sells.

    a)   Write a linear equation for her weekly salary, M in terms of the number of tubes of sunscreen sold, n. Then, use the equation to create a table of values for M and n using the linear formula.
Use $n = 64$, 76, 88, and 100.

    b)   What was Annabel's weekly pay if she sold 360 tubes of sunscreen last week?

    c)   If Annabel's weekly pay was $130, how many tubes of sunscreen did she sell that week?

Lesson 3.4   Solving for a Variable in a Two-Variable Linear Equation

Solve for _y_ in terms of _x_. Find _y_ when _x_ = −2.

1. $2(x + 1) = 7 - y$

2. $4 - 2y = 5x - 3$

3. $4(3x - y) = 10$

4. $7 - 3x = 2y - 0.6x$

5. $\frac{3}{2}x - \frac{1}{3}y = 4$

6. $1.2y + 3 = 0.36x$

Solve for _x_ in terms of _y_. Find _x_ when _y_ = 4.

7. $4y + x = 5(2x - y)$

8. $-2(x + 3y) = x + 6y$

9. $2.5\,(x - 2y) = 10$

10. $6y + 9 = \frac{2}{3}x$

11. $\frac{2(3x - 2)}{y} = 12$

12. $\frac{1}{4}(3 - 2x) = \frac{3y}{8}$

Name: _____ Date: _____

Solve. Show your work.

13. The diagram shows a quadrant of a circle
with a radius of *r* centimeters.

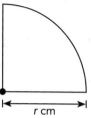

r cm

a) Express the perimeter of the quadrant, *P*, in terms of the radius *r*.

b) Express *r* in terms of *P*.

c) Find the radius if the perimeter is 50 centimeters. Use $\frac{22}{7}$ as an approximation for π.

14. A restaurant has *x* number of tables that seat four people and 5 tables which seat two people. The restaurant can seat *N* number of people.

a) Write a linear equation for *N*, number of people, in terms of *x*.

b) Solve for *x* in terms of *N*.

c) Find *X* when *N = 150*.

Name: _____   Date: _____

15. A formula for converting degrees Fahrenheit, F, to degrees Celsius, C is
$C = \frac{5}{9}(F - 32)$.

a) F in terms of C.

b) Create a table of F and C values for $C = 25$, 40, and 55.

c) If normal human body temperature is 37°C, what is this temperature in degrees Fahrenheit?

16. Mrs. Fields bought a sapling from a tree nursery and observed a linear growth of the sapling over a period of 6 months. She found the height of the sapling, H centimeters, and the time, t months is related by the linear equation $H = 2(4 + 3t)$.

a) Write an equation for t in terms of H.

b) Complete the table below.

Height (*H* centimeters)		20	26	
Time (*t* months)	1			4

c) Find H when $t = 6$.

d) How many months until the height of the sapling is 29 centimeters?

Name: _____ Date: _____

Solve. Show your work.

17. A square patio rug has side lengths of $\frac{1}{3}(x + 2)$ inches.

    a) Write a linear expression involving the perimeter of the square, P in terms of x.

    b) Solve for x in terms of P.

    c) Create a table of P and x values for $P = 4, 8, 12$, and 16.

    d) What is the value of x if the perimeter of the rug is 52 inches?

18. The interior angle, $A°$, of a regular polygon with n sides is represented by the linear equation $A = 180 - \frac{360}{n}$

    a) Solve for n in terms of A.

    b) Create a table of A and n values for $A = 60, 120, 140$, and 150.

    c) If the interior angles of a regular polygon measures 156°, find the number of sides of the polygon.

CHAPTER

 3 Brain @ Work

1. Solve the following equation for $\dfrac{p+3}{p-3} = \dfrac{3}{2} + 1$.

2. Mrs. Duffy roasted some almonds for her students. If she gives each student 7 almonds, she would have 26 almonds left. If she wanted to give each student 10 almonds, she would be short of 25 almonds. Using a linear equation, calculate the number of student in Mrs. Duffy's class. Then find the number of almonds that she roasted.

CHAPTER

Lines and Linear Equations

Lesson 4.1   Finding and Interpreting Slopes of Lines

Find the slope of each line.

1.

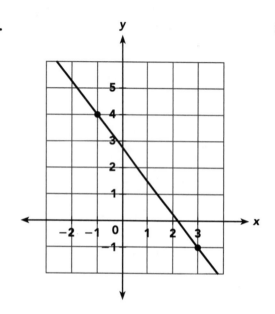

2.

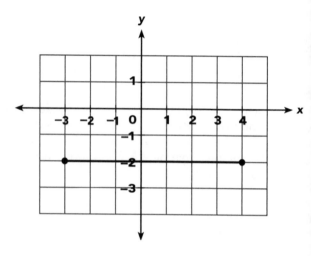

3.

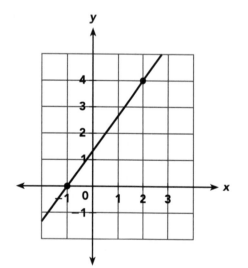

4.

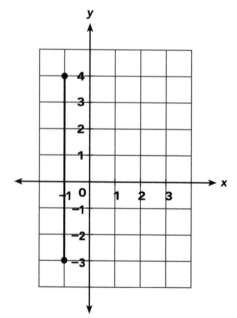

Name: _____   Date: _____

Find the slope of the line passing through each of the following pairs of points.

5. P (4, 5), Q (0, −3)

6. W (9, −2), X (9, 8)

7. R (−8, 2), S (−3, −3)

8. Y (7, 4), Z (3, 4)

Solve. Show your work.

9. An architect is designing an accesibility ramp to be used at the entrance of a convention center.

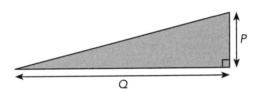

The table shows the different measures of P and Q, in feet, that the architect is considering.

Length of P (feet)	Length of Q (feet)	Slope of ramp
3	60	
5	50	
3	36	
2	30	

a) Complete the table above by computing the slope of the ramp for each set of measures.

b) Order the slopes from **a)** in descending order.

c) The Americans with Disabilities Act states that the maximum slope of a public ramp shall be 1 : 12. Which of the ramps in **a)** has a slope of 1 : 12?

Lesson 4.2   Understanding Slope-Intercept Form

Identify the y-intercept. Then calculate the slope using the points indicated.

1.

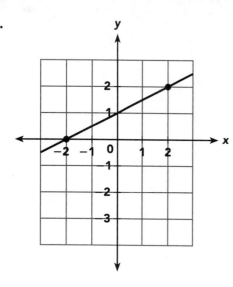

2.

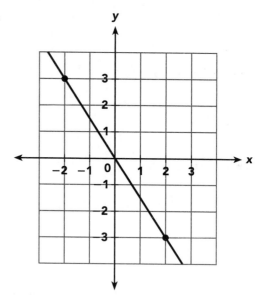

3.

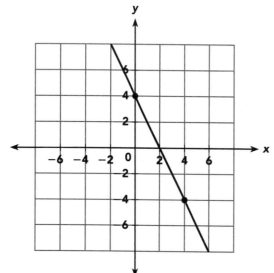

4.

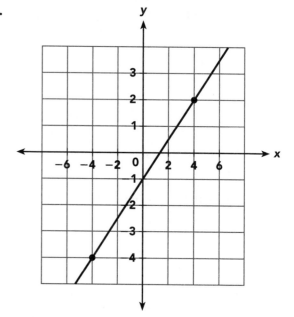

Name: _____   Date: _____

Write an equation in the form $y = mx$ or $y = mx + b$ for each line.

5.

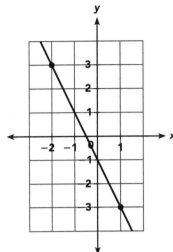

6.

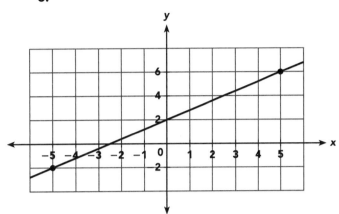

7.

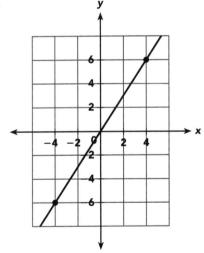

8.

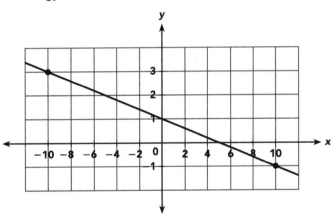

Graph each line using 1 grid square to represent 1 unit on both axes for the interval −5 to 5. Then write the equation for each line.

9. The line passes through the points (−2, −2) and (4, −2).

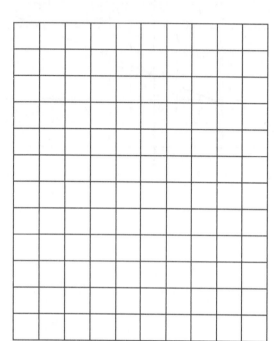

10. The line passes through the points (3, 5) and (3, −4).

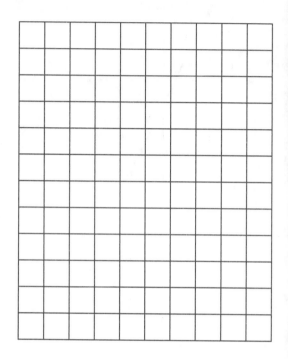

11. The line passes through the points (0, −4) and (0, 5).

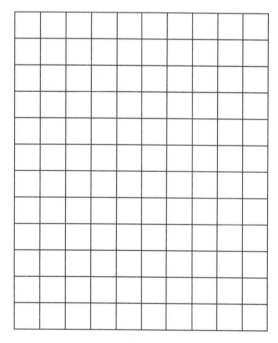

12. The line passes through the points (5, 0) and (−3, 0).

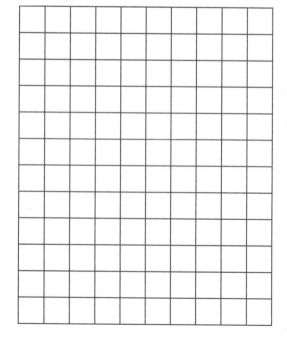

Lesson 4.3   Writing Linear Equations

For each equation, find the slope and the y-intercept of the graph of the equation.

1. $y = 4x - 7$

2. $y = -x + 3$

3. $4x - 3y = 9$

4. $-5x + 2y = 6$

Use the given slope and the y-intercept of a line to write an equation in slope-intercept form.

5. Slope, $m = \dfrac{2}{3}$
   y-intercept, $b = 1$

6. Slope, $m = -5$
   y-intercept, $b = 2$

Solve. Show your work.

7. Find an equation of the line that passes through the point $(0, -3)$ and has a slope of 2.

8. A line has slope $-\dfrac{3}{4}$ and passes through the point $(8, 3)$. Write an equation of the line.

9. A line has the equation $4x - 3y + 9 = 0$. Find an equation of a line parallel to this line that has a y-intercept of -1.

10. A line has the equation $5y + x = 10$. Find an equation of a line parallel to this line that has a y-intercept of 7.

Name: _____   Date: _____

Solve. Show your work.

11. A line has the equation $2y = -3x + 1$. Find an equation of a line parallel to this line that has a y-intercept of -2.

12. Find an equation of the line that passes through the point $(3, -5)$ and is parallel to $4x = 1 + 2y$.

13. Find an equation of the line that passes through the point $(7, 0)$ and is parallel to $7y = 6x - 14$.

14. Find an equation of the line that passes through the point $(-3, -2)$ and is parallel to $2x = 3 - 5y$.

15. Find an equation of the line that passes through the pair of points $(1, -6)$ and $(-4, 9)$.

16. Find an equation of the line that passes through the pair of points $(3, -10)$ and $(0, 11)$.

17. Find an equation of the line that passes through the pair of points $(-5, -9)$ and $(2, -7)$.

Name: _____ Date: _____

Lesson 4.4   Sketching Graphs of Linear Equations

For this practice, use 1 grid square to represent 1 unit on both axes for the interval −6 to 6.

Graph each of the following linear equations.

1. $y = \dfrac{2}{3}x + 2$

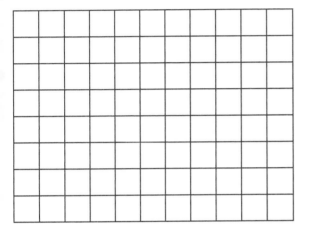

2. $y = \dfrac{3}{4}x - 5$

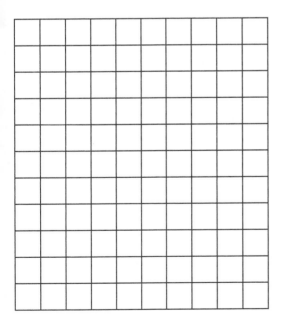

Graph each of the following linear equations.

3. $y = \dfrac{3}{5}x + 3$

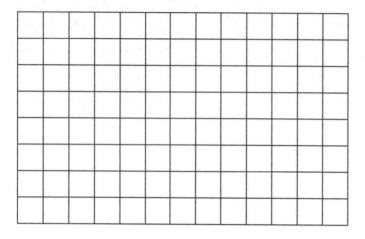

4. $y = 5 - 2x$

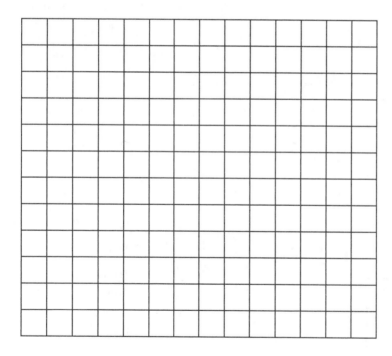

Graph each of the following linear equations.

5. $y = 2 - \frac{1}{6}x$

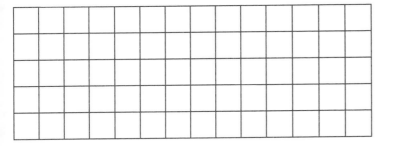

6. $y = \frac{4}{3}x - 4$

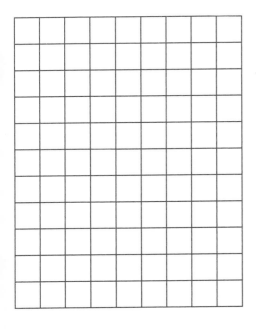

Graph each of the following linear equations.

7. Slope = 2; (2 , 5)

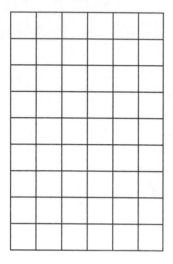

8. Slope = $-\dfrac{4}{5}$; (−5, 6)

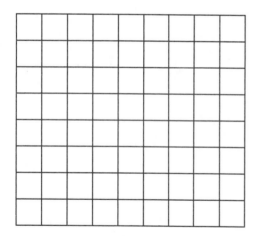

Name: _____   Date: _____

Graph each of the following linear equations.

9. Slope = −1; (3 , 2)

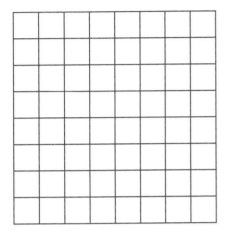

10. Slope = $\frac{3}{2}$; (−2, −4)

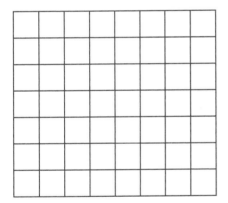

Lesson 4.5   Real-World Problems: Linear Equations

Solve. Show your work.

1. To rent a bike, Max pays a flat rate plus an hourly rental fee. The graph shows the amount, C dollars, he pays based on the number of hours, t, he uses the bike.

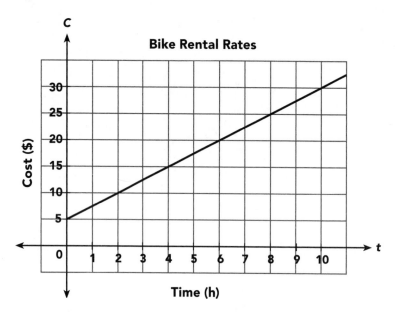

a) Find the vertical intercept of the graph and explain what information it gives about the situation.

b) Find the slope of the graph and explain what information it gives about the situation.

c) Find the amount Max pays to rent a bike for 6 hours.

Name: _____   Date: _____

Solve. Show your work.

2. The growth of two plant saplings A and B,
    were observed for a period of 6 months.
    The graph shows the linear growth of the
    saplings, in centimeters.

    a) Find the initial height of
        sapling A and sapling B.

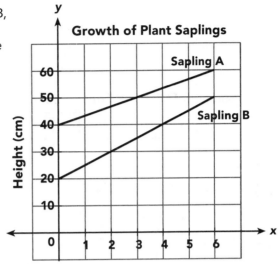

    b) Which sapling shows the greatest
        amount of growth during the
        6 month time period? Explain.

3. The graph shows the cost, *C*, of
    renting a concert hall for *t* hours.

    a) Find the vertical intercept of the
        graph and explain what information
        it gives about the situation.

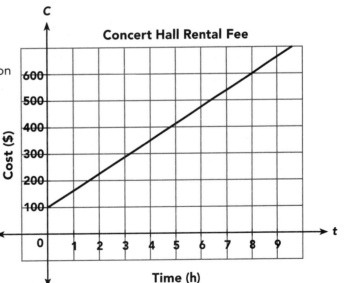

    b) Find the slope of the graph and
        explain what information it gives
        about the situation.

Name: _____   Date: _____

Solve. Show your work.

4. Two containers P and Q are filled with different amounts of water. Each container has a small hole. The graph shows the amount of water, V milliliters, left in each container after x minutes.

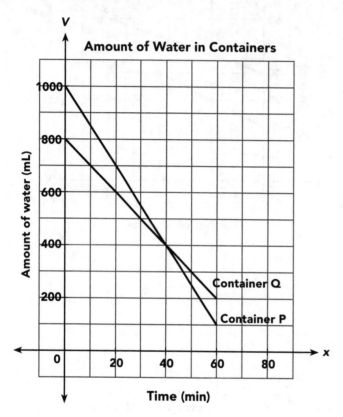

a) Find the initial amount of water in each container.

b) Which container has a bigger hole?

Solve. Show your work.

5. A candle is 9 inches long. Nelson lights the candle and records the length of the candle, y inches, for x hours.

Number of Hours Candle Burns (x hours)	0	1	2	3	4
Height of Candle (y inches)	9	7	5	3	1

a) Graph the relationship between candle height and time. Use 2 grid squares to represent 1 unit on the horizontal axis for the x-interval 0 to 4 and 1 grid square for 1 unit on the vertical axis for the y-interval 0 to 9.

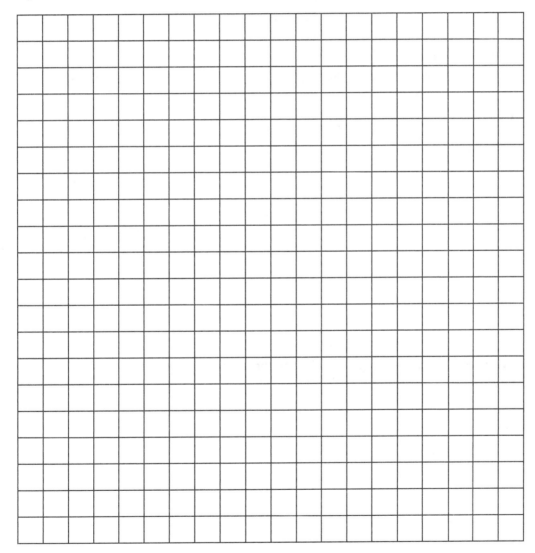

b) Find the vertical intercept of the graph and explain what information it gives about the situation.

c) Find the slope of the graph and explain what information it gives about the situation.

d) Write an equation relating the height of the candle and the number of hours it is lit.

Name: _____   Date: _____

Solve. Show your work.

1. A bus driver forgets to stop at a particular bus stop. When he realized it, he began to decelerate as he drove past that bus stop. The graph shows the speed of the bus, *y* meters per second, over *t* seconds.

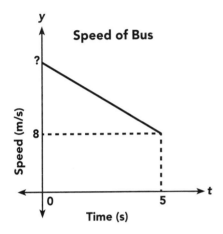

The bus is 50 meters beyond the stop and has slowed to 8 meters per second after 5 seconds.

a) Find the speed of the bus as it passes the bus stop.

b) Find the rate at which the bus slowed down, assuming it to be constant.

c) Write an equation to represent the speed of the bus, *y* meters per second, after *t* seconds.

Solve. Show your work.

2. Raymond drives his car from his home to the supermarket. The graph shows the speed of the car y, in kilometers per hour, he drives in t hours.

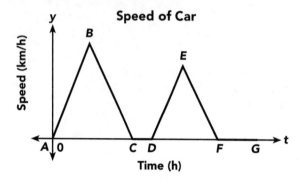

Describe the action of the car between the following points.

a) points A and B

b) points B and C

c) points C and D

d) points D and E

e) points E and F

f) points F and G

Cumulative Practice
for Chapters 3 to 4

Solve each equation. Show your work.

1. $3(2x - 4) - 7 = 23$

2. $5x - (8 - 3x) = 72$

3. $\dfrac{1}{6}(x + 3) - 4 = -3.2$

4. $2x - \dfrac{5}{9} = \dfrac{7x + 8}{9}$

Express each decimal as a fraction, without the use of a calculator.

5. $0.\overline{8}$

6. $0.\overline{54}$

Express each decimal as a fraction, without the use of a calculator.

7. $0.5\overline{3}$

8. $0.74\overline{1}$

Tell whether each equation has one solution, no solution, or an infinite number of solutions. Show your work.

9. $8 - 5x = 11x - 24$

10. $8x + 6 = 3\left(\dfrac{8}{3}x + 2\right)$

Tell whether each equation has one solution, no solution, or an infinite number of solutions. Show your work.

11. $14 - (12 - 4y) = \frac{1}{2}(8y + 3)$

12. $9y + 8 = 4\left(y - \frac{3}{4}\right)$

Find the value of y when x = −3.

13. $5x + 13 = 4 + y$

14. $7x - 3y = 6$

Find the value of y when x = −3.

15. $2x - 3y = \frac{1}{4}(x - 13)$

16. $\frac{2}{9}(3y + 4x) = 2x$

17. $\frac{5x - 3}{2y} = -\frac{3}{5}$

18. $\frac{7y - 4}{2} = 3x$

Solve for x in terms of y. Find x when y = 4.

19. $6x + 7y = 2(5x + y)$

20. $x + 9y = 6(x - y)$

Name: _____ Date: _____

Solve for *x* in terms of *y*. Find *x* when *y* = 4.

21. $\frac{3}{4}y - \frac{7}{8}x = 10$

22. $\frac{0.7(4x + 3)}{y} = 14$

23. $0.5(2x + y) = 12 - 3x$

24. $\frac{3y + x}{4} + \frac{y}{2} = 10$

For each graph, calculate the slope of the line using the points indicated. Then write an equation for the line in slope-intercept form.

25.

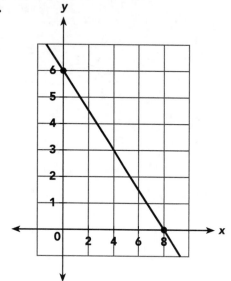

26.

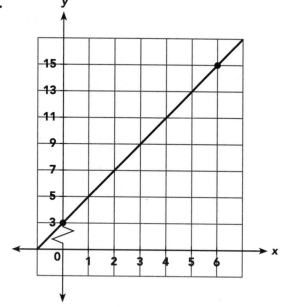

Name: _____ Date: _____

**For each graph, calculate the slope of the line using the points indicated.
Then write an equation for the line in slope-intercept form.**

27.

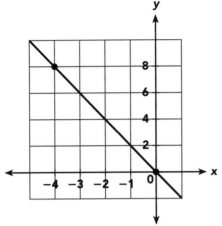

28.

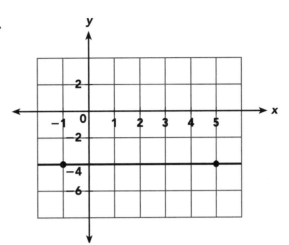

**For each equation, find the slope and the y-intercept of the graph of the
equation.**

29. $y = -\dfrac{4}{3}x$

30. $y = 9x - 4$

**Use the given slope and y-intercept of a line to write an equation in
slope-intercept form.**

31. slope, $m = 0$

y-intercept, $b = -\dfrac{2}{3}$

32. slope, $m = -\dfrac{1}{4}$

y-intercept, $b = 5$

Solve. Show your work.

33. Write an equation of the line parallel to $3x + 5 = 2y$ that has a y-intercept of -1.

34. A line has slope 7 and passes through the point (1, 9). Write an equation of the line.

35. Write an equation of the line that passes through the point (0, 0) and is parallel to $3y - 2x = 6$.

Solve. Show your work.

36. Write an equation of the line that passes through the point (0, 2) and is parallel
to $y + 8x = 0$.

**For each pair of points, write an equation of the line that passes through
the pair of points.**

37. (1, 6) and (5, 9)

38. (3, 2) and (7, −3)

Name: _____   Date: _____

Graph the given linear equation. Use 2 grid squares to represent 1 unit on both axes for the x – interval 0 to 2.

39. $2y + 3x = 1$

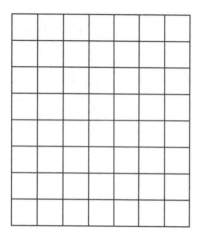

Graph the line with the given slope that passes through the given point. Use 1 grid square to represent 1 unit on both axes for the x – interval 0 to 12.

40. Slope: $\frac{1}{4}$; $(0, 3)$

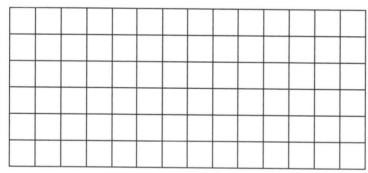

Name: _____   Date: _____

Solve. Show your work.

41. The diagram shows a vehicle lift. The vehicle is elevated such that the angles made by the legs of the lift to the ground are as given in the diagram. Write an equation in terms of x. Hence find the value of x.

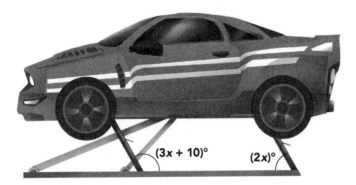

$(3x + 10)°$ $(2x)°$

42. Mr. and Mrs. Baker accompanied some children to a concert. Each adult ticket to the concert costs $7 and children were admitted at half the adult price.

a) Write a linear equation for the total cost, C in dollars, in terms of the number of children, n.

b) Solve for n in terms of C.

c) Calculate the number of children who attended the concert with Mr. and Mrs. Baker if the total cost was $35.

Solve. Show your work.

43. Gwen bought some boxes of mints at $6 each. She gave the cashier a $50 note and she received $y change.

a) Write a linear equation for the amount of change, y dollars, that she received in terms of the number of boxes of mints, n.

b) Solve for n in terms of y.

c) Calculate the number of boxes of mints that Gwen bought if she received $26 change.

d) Hilary also bought some boxes of the same mints. When she gave the cashier a $100 note, she also received the same $y change. Write a linear equation to find the number of boxes of mints, n, that each girl bought. Tell whether the equation has one solution, is inconsistent, or is an identity. Explain your reasoning.

Solve. Show your work.

44. The effort, *E* Newtons, and the load, *L* in Newtons, of a crane used to lift heavy objects are related by the equation $E = 0.4L + 50$.

a) Solve for *L* in terms of *E*.

b) Create a table of values for *E* and *L* when $E = 90N$, $130N$, $170N$ and $210N$.

Name: _____ Date: _____

Solve. Show your work.

45. Mobile providers *P* and *Q* each charge their customers *C* dollars. The charges consist of a monthly service fee plus a fixed per minute usuage charge.

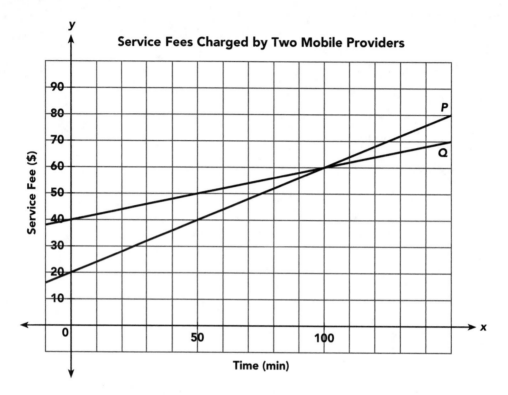

a) Find the monthly service fee that each mobile provider charges.

b) Which mobile provider charges a lesser per minute fee for the first 100 minutes?

Name: _____   Date: _____

Solve. Show your work.

46. A water tank filled to capacity has a leak. The graph shows the volume of water,
V in gallons, after *x* minutes.

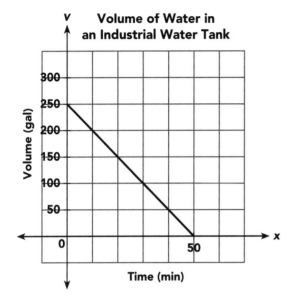

a)   Find the vertical intercept and explain what information it gives about the
     situation.

b)   Find the slope of the graph and explain what information it gives about
     the situation.

CHAPTER

Systems of Linear Equations

Lesson 5.1   Introduction to Systems of Linear Equations

**Solve the system of linear equations by making tables of values.
Each variable x is a positive integer less than 6.**

1. $x + 3y = 6$
   $2x - 3y = 3$

2. $2x - y = 1$
   $2x + 3y = 13$

3. $3x - y = 2$
   $2x = y$

4. $x + 3y = -4$
   $x + y = 2$

5. $2x + y = 10$
   $2x - y = 6$

6. $x - y = -2$
   $3x + y = 6$

7. $2y - x = 8$
   $2x - y = -1$

8. $3x + 4y = 15$
   $3x = y$

Name: _____   Date: _____

Solve by making a table of values. The values x and y are integers.

9. Jolene takes x minutes to fold a paper airplane and y minutes to fold a paper star. On a particular day, she folded 5 paper airplanes and 4 paper stars in 64 minutes. The following day, she folded 3 paper airplanes and 8 paper stars in 72 minutes. The related system of linear equations is:

   $5x + 4y = 64$
   $3x + 8y = 72$

   Solve the system of linear equations. Then find the time taken to fold a paper airplane and a paper star.

10. Janice is $2x$ years old and Jennifer is $3y$ years old. Janice is 3 times older than Jennifer. Two years later, their combined age will be 28 years. The related system of linear equations is:

    $2x = 9y$
    $2x + 3y = 24$

    Solve the system of equations. Then find the present age of Janice and of Jennifer.

11. Jack is training for a biathlon event. On one training day, he walked for 2 hours and cycled for an hour, covering 18 miles in the morning. In the afternoon, he walked for 2 hours and cycled for 3 hours, covering 42 miles. The related system of linear equations where x miles per hour is his walking speed and y miles per hour is his cycling speed, is:

    $2x + y = 18$
    $2x + 3y = 42$

    Solve the system of linear equations by making tables of values. Then find the difference between Jack's walking speed and cycling speed.

Lesson 5.2   Solving Systems of Linear Equations Using Algebraic Methods

Solve the systems of linear equations using the elimination method.

1. $3y - x = 2$
$3y + x = 16$

2. $x - 5y = 13$
$9y - x = -17$

3. $7q + 2p = 29$
$2p - q = 5$

4. $2w - 3v = 4$
$w + 3v = 29$

5. $2a - b = 6$
$3a + b = 19$

6. $6n - m = 3$
$3m - 6n = 15$

7. $8x + 6y = 14$
$6x + 3y = 6$

8. $4p + 5q = -18$
$3p - 10q = 69$

Name: _____ Date: _____

Solve the systems of linear equations using the substitution method.

9. $3a - b = 13$
$b = 2a - 7$

10. $5p + 3q = -7$
$q = -2p + 5$

11. $6c - b = 5$
$b - c = 5$

12. $2y - x = 3$
$y - x = 4$

13. $4h + k = 7$
$h + 2k = 7$

14. $3x + 2y = 36$
$5y - x = 39$

15. $5t + 2s = -3$
$7t - 2s = 15$

16. $5x + 4y = -26$
$5 - x = -6y$

Name: _____ Date: _____

Solve the systems of linear equations using the substitution method or the elimination method. Explain why you choose the method.

17. $3x + 5y = 35$
$6x - 4y = -28$

18. $7m - 2n = -13$
$2n - 5m = 11$

19. $9m + 4n = 38$
$2m = 5n - 21$

20. $5w - 4v = 1$
$v = 6w + 14$

21. $2h + 9k = 19$
$5h - 5k = 20$

22. $5y + 9 = 3x$
$3x - 2y = 18$

23. $3b + 4c = -6$
$7b + 16c = -34$

24. $7p - q = 18$
$3p + 4q = 21$

Lesson 5.3 Real-World Problems: Systems of Linear Equations

Solve using systems of linear equations.

1. Jenny purchased 26 magazines for her project research at a total cost of $134. The art related magazines cost $4 each, while the science related magazines cost $7 each. Find the number of art related magazines and science related magazines purchased.

2. A total of 95 theme park tickets were sold for $960. Each adult ticket cost $12 and each child's ticket cost $9. Find the number of adult tickets and the number of children's tickets sold.

3. Adam bought 5 packets of roasted peanuts and 3 packets of beef jerky for $37.80. Joe bought 3 packets of roasted peanuts and 2 packets of beef jerky for $23.87. Find the cost of a packet of roasted peanuts and a packet of beef jerky.

Solve using systems of linear equations.

4. Half a dozen glass containers and 2 plastic containers can store up to 180 wheat crackers. Four glass containers can store a total of 25 more wheat crackers than 5 plastic containers. How many wheat crackers can each glass container and each plastic container store?

5. The diagram shows an equilateral triangle of a face of a crystal solid with the given sides. Find the values of x and y.

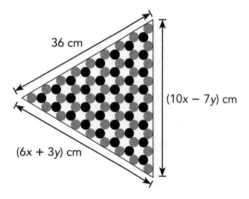

36 cm

(10x − 7y) cm

(6x + 3y) cm

6. Mrs. Quincy plans to build a rectangular sandbox for her grandson, Timothy. She has 26 meters of wood for the perimeter of the sandbox. The length of the sandbox is to be 3 meters longer than the breadth.

   a) Write a system of linear equations relating the length *l* and width *w* of the perimeter of the sandbox.

   b) Find the dimensions of the rectangular sandbox.

Name: _____   Date: _____

Solve using systems of linear equations.

7. A vending machine only accepts dimes and quarters. There are 85 coins in the machine with a total value of $16.75. How many of each coin are in the machine?

8. At a fund raising event, a booth was set up to sell handmade cards and photo frames. On the first day, 3 cards and 9 photo frames were sold for a total of $75. The next day, 8 cards and 5 photo frames were sold for a total of $67. Find the selling price of a card and the selling price of a photo frame.

9. Ben took a mathematics quiz where he had to solve the following questions.

a) The sum of two numbers is 31. Twice the larger number is 7 more than 3 times the smaller number. What are the numbers?

b) The sum of a number and twice a second number is 14. When the second number is subtracted from the first number, the difference is 2. Find the two numbers.

Name: _____ Date: _____

Solve using systems of linear equations.

10. A tennis club charges an entry fee for the players at the club. The table below shows the money received on a particular Saturday and Sunday.

Day	Number of Senior Players	Number of Junior Players	Entry Fees Charged ($)		Amount of Money Received ($)
			For Seniors	For Juniors	
Saturday	35	20			310
Sunday	55	45	x	y	555

How much is the entry fee for each senior and each junior?

11. The table shows the number of words that can be printed on a page for two given font sizes.

Font Size	Number of Words on a Page
Small	1,150
Large	850

Jacob needs to print a document with a total of 12,600 words on exactly 12 pages. Find the number of pages in the document that should be printed in small font and the number of pages that should be printed in large font.

12. Kelly, a chemist, was asked to prepare 24 gallons of a solution that is 50% acidic by mixing a solution that is 20% acidic with another solution that is 70% acidic. How much of each solution should she use?

Name: _____   Date: _____

Lesson 5.4   Solving Systems of Linear Equations
by Graphing

**For this practice, unless otherwise states, use 1 grid square to represent
1 unit on both axes for the interval −8 to 8.**

1. **a)**   Complete the tables of values for the system of linear equations.

$x - y = 1$ $x + 2y = 4$

x	0	1	2
y	−1		

x	0	1	2
y	2		

   b)   Graph $x - y = 1$ and $x + 2y = 4$ on the same coordinate plane. Find the
point of intersection.

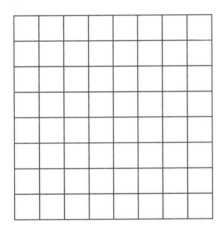

   c)   Use the graph to solve the system of linear equations.

$x - y = 1$
$x + 2y = 4$

2. a) Graph $3x - 5y = 4$ and $x + 2y = 5$ on the same coordinate plane.

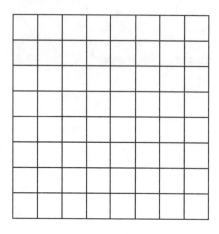

b) Find the point of intersection of the graphs.

c) Use the graph to solve the system of linear equations.

$3x - 5y = 4$
$x + 2y = 5$

3. a) Graph $x - 3y = 5$ and $3x + 2y = 4$ on the same coordinate plane.

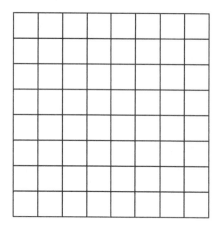

b) Find the point of intersection of the graphs.

c) Use the graph to solve the system of linear equations.

$x - 3y = 5$
$3x + 2y = 4$

Solve the systems of equations using the graphical method.

4. $x = 5y$
$y = x - 4$

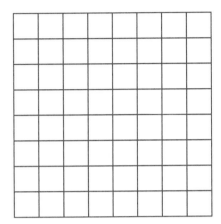

5. $y = 6$
$y = 4x + 4$

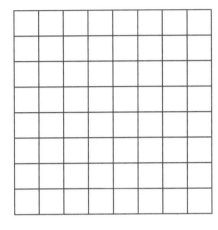

6. $x = 4$
$y = 3x - 5$

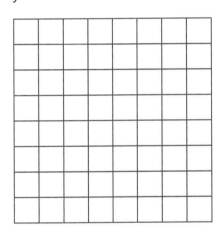

7. $2y = -x + 7$
$y = 2x + 1$

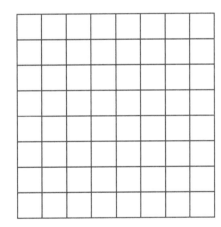

8. $x + 2y = -1$
$4x + y = 3$

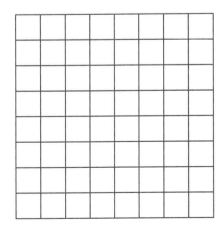

9. $5y - x = 15$
$x - 3y = -9$

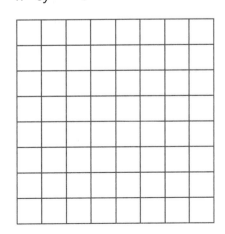

Solve. Show your work.

10. Two different vendors rent their campgrounds to various schools for retreat programs. The rental charges consist of a fixed cost. The variable cost depends on the number of campers. The charges by each vendor is represented by $C = 120 + 5n$ and $C = 90 + 7n$ where C is the cost, in dollars, and n is the number of campers.

    a) 🖩 Solve the system of linear equations using your graphing calculator.

    b) For how many campers will the cost of the rental charge be the same for each vendor?

11. Two vehicles are moving along a straight road in the same direction. Their motions are described by the linear equations $d = 5t + 45$ and $d - 15t = 25$, where t hours is the time and d miles is the distance.

    a) 🖩 Solve the system of linear equations using your graphing calculator.

    b) When will the two vehicles meet?

12. Weights are attached to two different springs. The length of stretch and the amount of weight attached to the spring are described by the linear equations $L = 3w + 7$ and $L = 5w + 3$, where L inches is the length of the spring stretched and w pounds is the weight attached to the spring.

    a) 🖩 Solve the system of linear equations using your graphing calculator.

    b) For which weight amounts will the springs stretch the same number of inches?

Name: _____   Date: _____

Lesson 5.5   Inconsistent and Dependent Systems
of Linear Equations

Graph the system of linear equations on a coordinate grid. State whether the system of equations is inconsistent or dependent.

1. $5x + 2y = 16$
    $10x + 4y = 22$

2. $12x + 4y = 20$
    $3x + y = 5$

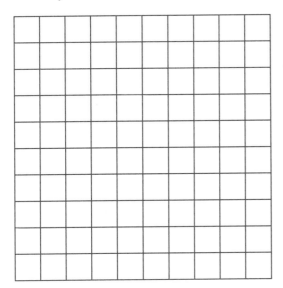
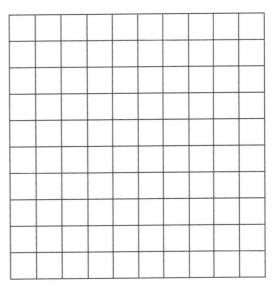

Graph the system of linear equations on a graphing calculator. State whether the system of linear equations is inconsistent or dependent.

3. $2x + y = 11$
    $5y = 10x - 5$

4. $2x + 2y = 5$
    $10x + 10y = 45$

State whether each system of linear equations is inconsistent, dependent, or has a unique solution. Justify each answer. Solve each system of linear equations if possible.

5. $8x + 4y = 14$
$2x + y = 28$

6. $12x - 3y = 9$
$4x - y = 3$

7. $-24x + 8y = 4$
$-6x + 2y = 17$

8. $3x + 4y = 22$
$6x - 8y = 28$

9. $4x + 9y = 7$
$16x + 36y = 28$

10. $x + 5y = 17$
$2x + 10y = 11$

11. $12x + 36y = 54$
$6x + 18y = 27$

12. $2x + 3y = 5$
$14x + 21y = 35$

Name: _____   Date: _____

Solve. Show your work.

13. Melissa reserved a two-night stay at a lodge inclusive of 3 meals for $185. Angela reserved the same lodge for a four-night stay, inclusive of 6 meals for $350.

    a) Write a system of linear equations to find the cost of a one-night stay and one meal at the lodge.

    b) State with reasons whether the system of equations has a unique solution, is inconsistent, or is independent.

    c) What does this tell you about the reservations made by Melissa and Angela?

14. Mr. Henderson bought some wooden planks of different lengths.

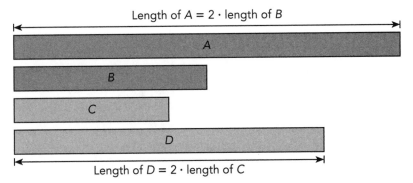

Length of $A = 2 \cdot$ length of B

Length of $D = 2 \cdot$ length of C

When he places planks A and D end-to-end, the total length is 16 inches.
When he places planks B and C end-to-end, the total length is 8 inches.

    a) Write a system of equations to find the length of the wooden plank B and the length of wooden plank C.

    b) State with reasons whether the system of equations has a unique solution, is inconsistent, or is independent.

Name: _____   Date: _____

 **Brain @ Work**

1. Brendan was given this riddle to find the number in the password of his friend's cell phone.

    It is a 2-digit number.
    The sum of the digits of the number is 11.
    When the digits are reversed, the value of the number increases by 9.
    What is the number in my password?

2. The digits 1 through 8 are to be placed in the circles so that the sum of the numbers on each side of the figure is 15. Fill in the appropriate number in each circle.

    Note: Each number can only be used once.

    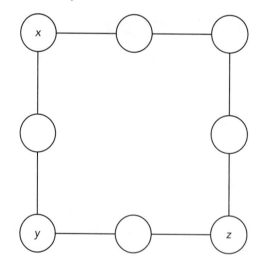

    (Hint: x satisfies the equation $-4(x - 2) = 2 - 2x$,
    y satisfies the equation $9 + 2(y - 3) - 3(y - 2) = 1$ and
    z satisfies the equation $\left(\dfrac{z}{3} + \dfrac{1}{2} = \dfrac{5}{2} \right)$.

CHAPTER

Functions

Lesson 6.1   Understanding Relations and Functions

Given the relation described, identify the input and the output.

1. Fred wants to know his weekly salary when he works in a certain
   number of hours per week at a constant hourly pay rate.

2. In an experiment, Josie wants to find out how the length of a shadow changes
   during different times of the day.

3. Mr. Warren wants to know how many miles he can drive his car for various
   gallons of gasoline in his car's fuel tank.

Based on the mapping diagram, state the type of relation.

4.
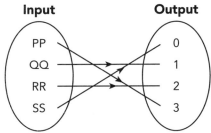

5.
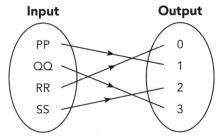

Draw a mapping diagram to represent each relation. Then identify each type of relation.

6. Mrs. Manuel carried out a survey to find out the favorite colors of her students so that she could hand make some personalized-colored bookmarks as student gifts. The table shows the color preference of each student in her class.

Input, Favourite Colors	Red	Blue	Yellow	Violet	Green
Output, Number of Students	6	10	3	3	3

7. The table shows the number of signatures collected each day for seven days by a citizen wanting to run for town council.

Input, Number of Signatures	55	43	55	30	75	55	62
Output, Day	1	2	3	4	5	6	7

Draw a mapping diagram to represent the relation between the number of signatures collected on each day. Identify the type of relation between the numbers of signatures and the day.

Name: _____   Date: _____

Tell whether each statement is True or False. Explain.

8. A one-to-one relation is always a function.

9. A function is a special type of relation.

10. When Martha clicks on any of the icons in a folder on her computer, it will open only the file that she clicks on. She says the folder represents a function.

11. In a relation where the input is the age of students in a class and the output is the height of the students, the relation is a function.

Identify the type of relation in each mapping diagram. Then tell whether the relation is a function. Explain.

12.

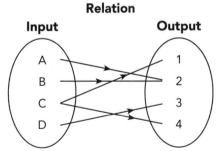

13.

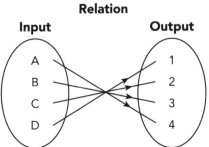

Tell whether the relation represented by each graph is a function. Explain.

14.

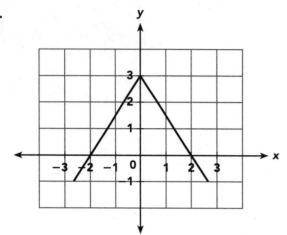

15.

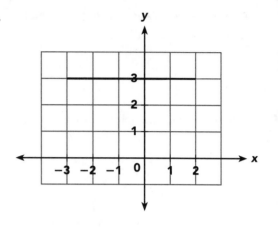

16.

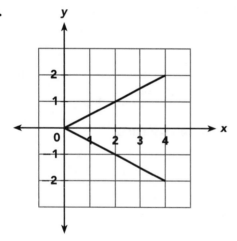

17.

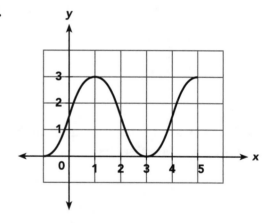

Name: _____   Date: _____

Tell whether the relation described is a function. Use a graph to support your answer.

18. Howard surveyed some students to see if the weekly allowance they received from their parents depended on the age of the student. The table shows the age, x years, and the amount y dollars, of weekly allowance.

Input, Age (x years)	12	12	13	14	14
Output, Allowance (y dollars)	10	13	13	15	15

Use 1 unit on the horizontal axis to represent 1 year for the x interval from 11 to 14 and 1 unit on the vertical axis to represent $2 for the y interval from 0 to 15.

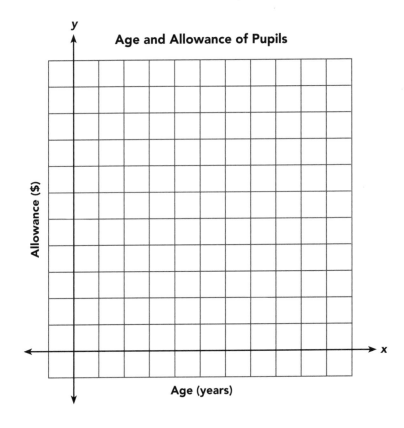

Age and Allowance of Pupils

Name: _____   Date: _____

19. Michael plans to save a quarter every day. Use 1 unit on the horizontal axis to represent 1 day for the x interval from 1 to 7 and 1 unit on the vertical axis to represent 25 cents for the y axis from 0 to 175.

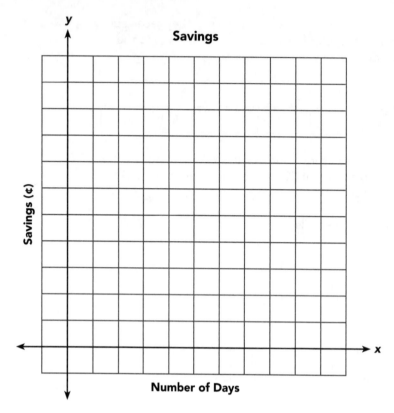

Name: _____   Date: _____

Solve. Show your work.

20. The table shows the number of available parking spots in each five parking garages.

Input, Garage	A	B	C	D	E
Output, Number of Available Parking Spots	425	510	418	425	608

a) Draw a mapping diagram to represent the relation between each and the number of available parking spots.

b) From the mapping diagram, identify the relation between the garages and the number available parking spots.

c) Tell whether the relation represented by the mapping diagram is a function. Explain.

Name: _____   Date: _____

21. The table shows the number of shoes manufactured by each of five factories and the production cost incurred during the week.

Factory	A	B	C	D	E
Number of Shoes Produced	674	480	535	605	674
Production Cost	$10,110	$7,200	$8,025	$9,075	$10,110

a) Draw a mapping diagram to represent the relation between the factories and the number of shoes produced.

b) From the mapping diagram, identify the relation between the factory and the number of shoes produced. Then tell whether the relation represented by the mapping diagram is a function. Explain.

c) Draw a mapping diagram to represent the relation between the production costs incurred by the factories and the number of shoes produced. Identify the relation between the production cost and the number of shoes produced. Then tell whether the relation represented by the mapping diagram is a function. Explain.

Lesson 6.2   Representing Functions

Write a verbal description of each function. Then write an algebraic equation for the function.

1. Laura can type 75 words per minute on a computer keyboard.
   The number of words she can type, N, is a function of the amount of time,
   t minutes, she spends at the computer keyboard.

2. When Melissa goes on vocation, she boards her dog at a kennel. The kennel
   charges a flat fee of $50 and a daily rate of $10. The total amount Melissa pays
   for her dog to stay at the kennel, y dollars, is a function of the number of days
   that she boards the dog, d.

Write an algebraic equation for each function. Then construct a table of x and y values for the function.

3. Maria and her friends are making beaded bracelets to raise funds for their
   mission trip. Each bracelet is made up of 12 beads. The total number of beads
   needed, y, is a function of the number of bracelets they make, x.

4. A tank contains 72 gallons of water. A pump rated at 5 gallons per minute, is
   used to transfer water from the tank to a mixing vessel. The amount of water in
   the tank, A, is a function of the amount of time the pump is in use, t minutes.

Each of the following graphs represents a function. Write an algebraic equation to represent the function.

5.

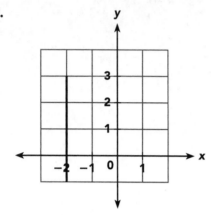

6.

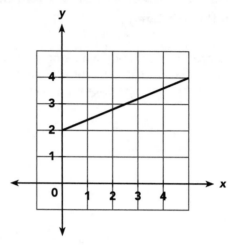

Use the table of values to plot a graph to represent the function.

7. The table shows the number of hanging brackets, y, needed to hang x paintings in an art gallery. Use 1 unit on the horizontal axis to represent 1 painting for the x interval and 1 unit on the vertical axis to represent 3 brackets for the y interval.

Number of Paintings (x)	0	2	5	8
Number of Brackets (y)	3	9	18	27

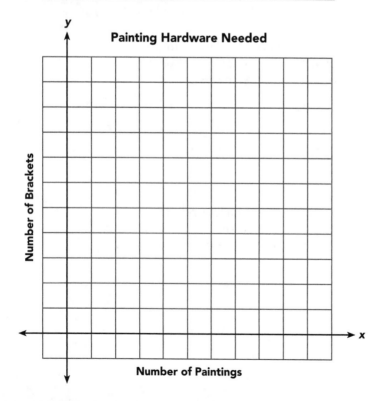

Painting Hardware Needed

Name: _____   Date: _____

Use the table of values to plot a graph to represent the function. Then write an algebraic equation for the function.

8. A dancing studio charges a $35 registration fee for class enrollment plus a per class fee. The dance class Marissa plans to take is $70 per hour. The table shows the total cost, y dollars, as a function of the number of class hours, x. Use 1 unit on the horizontal axis to represent 1 hour for the x interval and 1 unit on the vertical axis to represent $35 for the y axis.

Number of Class Hours (x)	0	1	2	3	4	5	6
Total Cost ($)	35	105	175	245	315	385	455

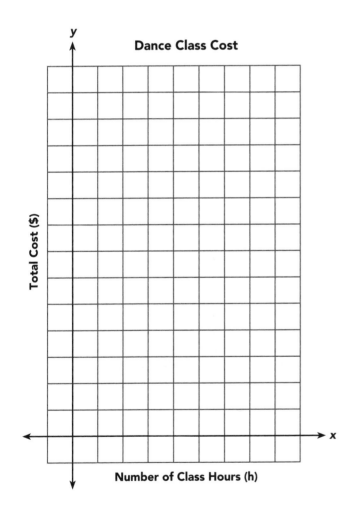

Dance Class Cost

Total Cost ($)

Number of Class Hours (h)

Solve. Show your work.

9. The graph shows the number of sheets of paper, *y*, remaining in the input paper tray of a photocopy machine as a function of the time the machine is operational, *x* minutes.

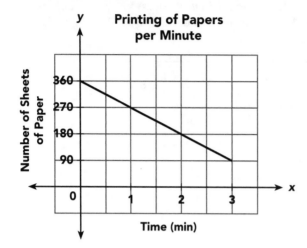

a)   Write an equation in slope-intercept form to represent the function.

b)   What information do the values for slope and *y*-intercept give you about the function?

10. Jason had a prepaid movie card with a value of $45. Every time he watches a movie, $7.50 is deducted from the value of his card. The amount of money remaining on his card, y dollars, is a function of the number of movies he watches, *x*.

a)   Write a verbal description of the function and then write an algebraic equation for the function.

b)   Construct a table of *x* and *y* values for the function in **a)**. Use values of *x* from 0 to 6.

c) Use the table of values in **b)** to plot a graph to represent the function. Use 1 unit on the horizontal axis to represent 1 movie watched for the *x* interval from 0 to 6 and 1 unit on the vertical axis to represent $5 for the *y* interval from 0 to 45.

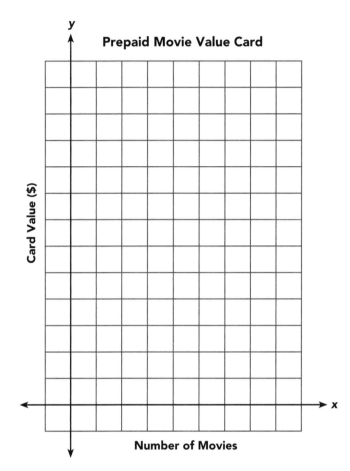

Prepaid Movie Value Card

Card Value ($)

Number of Movies

Lesson 6.3   Understanding Linear and Nonlinear Functions

Tell whether each table of values represents a linear or non-linear function.

1.

x	1	3	5	7
y	2	18	50	98

2.

x	−1	3	7	11
y	−4	8	20	32

3.

x	−4	0	4	8
y	4	5	6	7

4.

x	−2	0	2	4
y	−8	4	−8	−14

Tell whether each graph represents a linear function. If so, find the rate of change.

5.

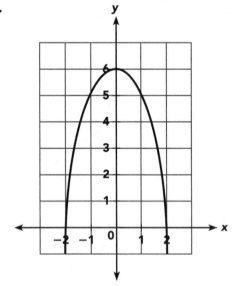

6.

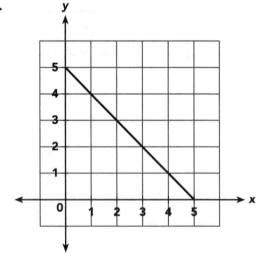

Tell whether each function is linear or nonlinear. Then tell whether the function is increasing or decreasing.

7.

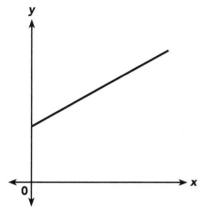

8.

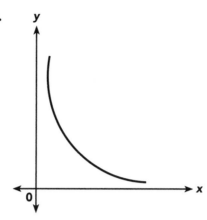

9.

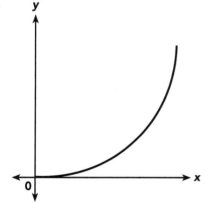

10.

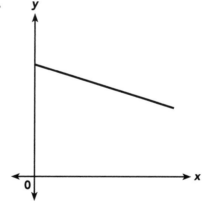

Describe the function. Sketch a graph for the function.

11. A hot beverage dispenser machine with a capacity of 3.3 liters dispenses 110 milliliters cup of a beverage into a mug for every press of the dispense button. The total amount of beverage left in the dispenser, V liters, is a function of the number of presses on the dispense button, p.

a) Give the least possible input and the corresponding output value. Tell whether the function is increasing or decreasing. Then tell whether the function is linear or nonlinear. Explain.

b) Sketch a graph for the function.

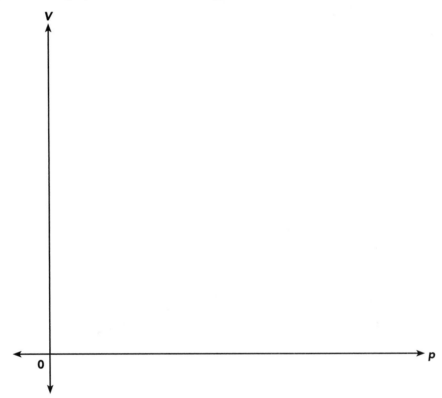

Name: _____   Date: _____

Describe the function. Sketch a graph for the function.

12. An internet file can be downloaded at *s* kilobytes per second via a broadband
connection. The total amount of data downloaded, *D* kilobytes, is a function of
the speed at which the data can be downloaded, *s*.

a) Give the least possible input value and the corresponding output value.
Tell whether the function is increasing or decreasing. Then tell whether the
function is linear or nonlinear. Explain.

b) Sketch a graph for the function.

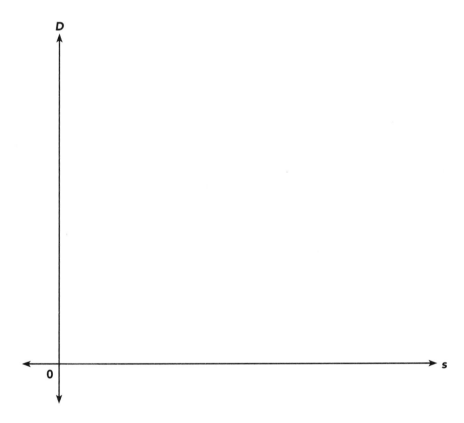

Name: _____   Date: _____

Solve. Show your work.

13. The table shows the volume of a cube, V cubic centimeters, as a function of its side length, x centimeters.

Input, Side Length (x centimeters)	0	1	2	3	4
Output, Volume (V cubic centimeters)	0	1	8	27	64

a) Tell whether the function is linear or nonlinear. Then tell whether the function is increasing or decreasing. Explain.

b) Graph the table of values and draw a curve through the points. Use 1 unit on the horizontal axis to represent 1 unit for the x interval from 0 to 4 and 1 unit on the vertical axis to represent 10 cubic centimeters for the y interval from 0 to 64. Do the coordinates of every point on the curve make sense for the function? Explain.

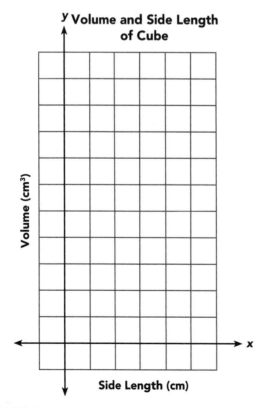

y Volume and Side Length of Cube

Volume (cm³)

Side Length (cm)

x

Name: _____   Date: _____

14. The table shows the age of Kelly's father, *y*, as a function of Kelly's age, *x*.

Input, Kelly's Age (x years)	0	4	8	12	16	20
Output, Kelly's Father's Age (y years)	25	33	41	49	57	65

a) Tell whether the function is linear or nonlinear. Then tell whether the function is increasing or decreasing. Explain.

b) Graph the table of values and draw a line through the points. Use 1 unit on the horizontal axis to represent 4 years for the *x* interval from 0 to 20 and 1 unit on the vertical axis to represent 8 years for the *y* interval from 25 to 65. Do the coordinates of every point on the line make sense for the function? Explain.

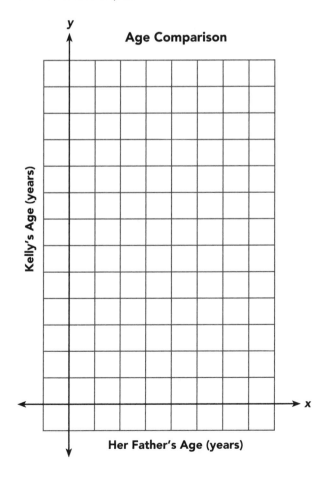

Lesson 6.4   Comparing Two Functions

Tell whether the equation $y = \dfrac{5}{2}x - 3$ **can represent each of the following functions.**

1.

x	−2	0	2	4
y	8	3	−2	13

2.

x	−2	0	2	4
y	−8	−3	2	7

3.

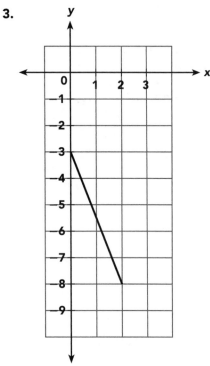

4.

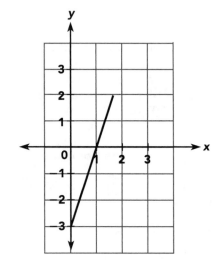

Tell whether each function can represent the table of values.

x	−1	2	5
y	7	−5	−17

5. $y = 4x - 3$

6. $y = -4x + 3$

7.

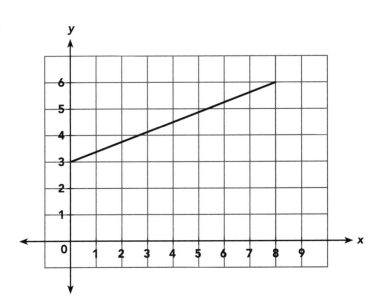

Tell whether each function represents the verbal description.

Marianna has 50 stamps in her collection. When she joins a philatelic club, she receives 12 stamps every month from the club. y represents the total number of stamps she has and x represents the number of months.

8. $y = 50 + 12x$

9. $y = 12 + 50x$

10.

Number of Months (x)	3	7	11
Total Number of Stamps (y)	86	134	182

Solve. Show your work.

11. Two identical water tanks A and B contain some water. Water is added to each tank by way of dedicated water faucets. The functions that relate each tank's total volume of water, V gallons, to the number of minutes, t, that each faucet is running, are as follows:
Tank A: $V = 80 + 25t$
Tank B: $V = 100 + 15t$

a) Use a verbal description to compare the two functions.

Name: _____ Date: _____

b) Graph the two functions on the same coordinate plane. Use 1 unit on the horizontal axis to represent 1 minute for the x interval from 0 to 6 and 1 unit on the vertical axis to represent 25 gallons for the y axis from 80 to 230. For each function, draw a line through the points.

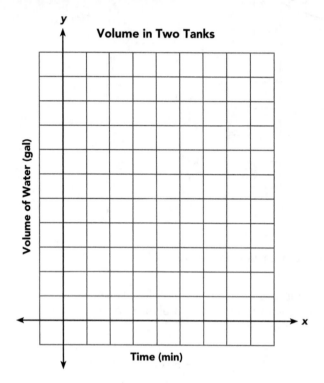

c) Which tank is most likely to be filled to capacity first? Explain

Name: _____ Date: _____

12. You have two options for paying a lawn service. Both options involve paying
a flat fee and then paying an additional hourly charge for labor. For each
function, the total amount you would pay, y dollars, is a function of the number
of hours worked, t.

Option A

Number of Hours Worked (*t* hours)	2	3	4
Total Fee (*y* dollars)	45	55	65

Option B   A basic rate of $20 plus $12 per hour

a) Write an algebraic equation to represent each function.

b) Use a verbal description to compare the two functions.

13. A factory needs to churn at least 5,000 pounds of butter daily. The manager
of the factory is trying to decide which machine to run to achieve this output.
The functions shown describe the amount of time, *t* minutes, it takes to churn *y*
pounds of butter for two different machines, A and B.

Machine A
The function is $y = 3,000 - 60t$.
The initial value 3,000 represents
the mass of each batch of butter
to be churned.

Machine B

Mass of Butter to be Churned

a) Write an algebraic equation to represent the function for Machine *B*.

b) Which machine would you recommend that the manager use for the
churning operation? Explain.

CHAPTER

6 Brain @ Work

1. The owner of a baseball team hires a firm to produce inspirational posters to commemorate their 10th championship title. The firm charges a basic fee of $500 and an additional $2 for each poster produced. The cost, *C* dollars, is a function of the number of posters produced, *p*.

   a) Write an algebraic equation to represent the function, C.

   b) Graph the function in **a)**. Use 1 unit on the horizontal axis to represent 100 posters for the *x* interval from 0 to 600 and 2 units on the vertical axis to represent $500 for the *y* axis from 0 to 2,000. Draw a line through the points.

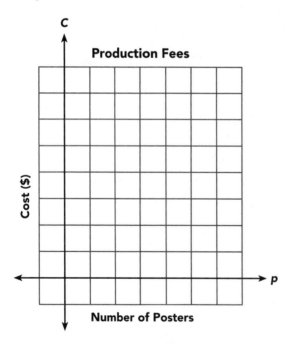

   The owner of the baseball team plans to sell the posters during the next game for $4 each. The profit, *P* dollars, is a function of the number of posters sold, *p*.

   c) Given that profit is the difference between revenue received from the sale of p posters and the cost of producing p posters, write an algebraic equation to represent the function *P*.

d) Graph the function in **c)**. Use 1 unit on the horizontal axis to represent 100 posters for the *x* interval from 0 to 600 and 1 unit on the vertical axis to represent $100 for the *y* axis from −100 to 800. Draw a line through the points.

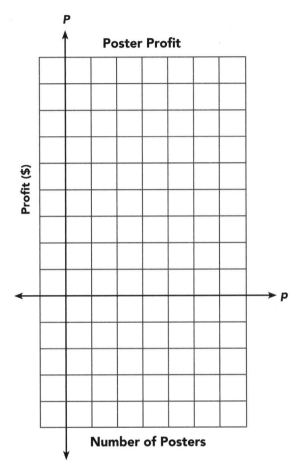

e) How many posters must be sold for the owner to break even?

Cumulative Practice
for Chapters 5 to 6

**Solve each system of linear equations by making tables of values.
Each variable x is a positive integer less than 4.**

1. $4x + 3y = 13$
   $2x - 7y = 15$

2. $y - 4x = 16$
   $6y + x = 46$

**Solve each system of linear equations by using the elimination or
substitution method. Explain your choice of method.**

3. $x - y + 5 = 0$
   $x + 4y = 25$

4. $6x + 4y = 64$
   $2x + 3y = 23$

5. $\frac{1}{2}x + y = 1$

   $\frac{1}{4}x - 2y = 8$

6. $4x - y = -3$
   $x + y = 8$

Name: _____   Date: _____

Solve each system of linear equations by using the graphical method.
Use 1 grid square on both axes to represent 1 unit for the interval from 0 to 7.

7. $3x - 2y = 17$
   $x - 2y = 7$

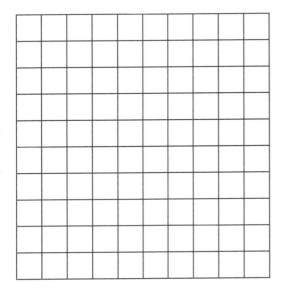

8. $7x - 3y = 15$
   $x + 2y = 7$

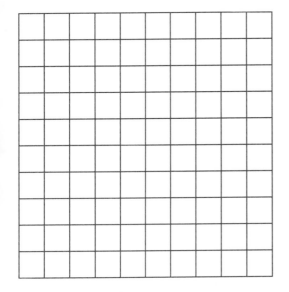

Name: _____   Date: _____

Identify whether each system of linear equations is inconsistent or dependent. Justify your answer.

9. $x + 2y = 5$
$2x + 4y = 10$

10. $\frac{2}{3}x - y = 1$
$2x - 3y = 7$

11. $\frac{1}{3}x - 3y = 1$
$x = 9y + 8$

12. $7x - 14y - 28 = 0$
$3x = 12 - 6y$

Name: _____ Date: _____

Tell whether the relation in each mapping diagram, table, or graph is a function. Explain.

13. Student   Relation   Means of
                          Transport
                          to School

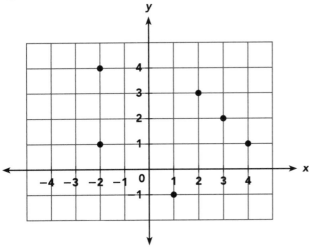

Nicky
Joyce
Max
Loraine

Car
Bus
Cycle

14.

Input, Wheat Cracker Stall	Output, Number of Wheat Crackers sold
A	10
B	30
C	55
D	110

15.

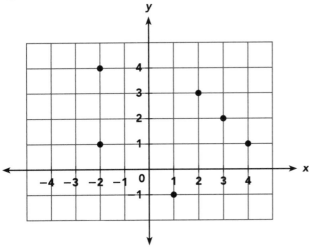

16.

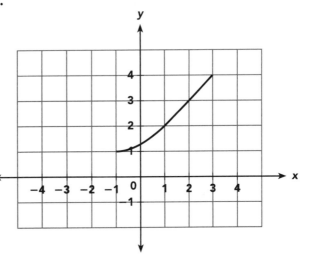

Write an algebraic equation for each function.

17. Grace is traveling at a constant speed of 75 miles per hour. The distance she travels, x miles, is a function of the amount of time she takes to travel, t hours.

18. A cylindrical container initially contains 8 liters of water. Water is then poured into the container at a rate of 2 liters per minute. The total amount of water in the container, y liters, is a function of the number of minutes that water is poured into the container, x.

Tell whether each table, equation, or graph represents a linear function. If so, find the rate of change. Then tell whether the function is increasing or decreasing.

19.

x	2	6	10	14
y	8	24	40	56

20. The area of a square, A square inches, is a function of its perimeter, p inches where $A = \dfrac{1}{16}p^2$.

Solve. Show your work.

21. Mr. Roderick recorded the number of questions students answered correctly on a quiz and their corresponding quiz score.

Number of Questions Answered Correctly	1	2	3	4	5
Quiz Score	3	6	9	12	15

Draw a mapping diagram to represent the relation between the number of questions answered correctly and the total score obtained. Is this relation a function? Explain.

Name: _____   Date: _____

Solve. Show your work.

22. Mr. Nelson is 9 times as old as his son, John. In 9 years' time, Mr. Nelson will be three times as old as his son. How old is each of them now?

23. The diagram shows a motif made up of equilateral triangles and regular hexagons. Some of the measures of the side lengths, in inches, are indicated in the diagram.

a) Find the values of x and y.

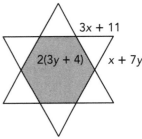

$3x + 11$

$2(3y + 4)$ $x + 7y$

b) Find the length of each side of the regular hexagon.

24. Priscilla joined a book club that charges a membership fee of $30. The cost of each book purchased by a member is $10. The total amount of money she spends, y dollars, is a function of the number of books she buys, n.

a)   Write an algebraic equation for the function.

b)   Graph the function and draw a line through the points. Use 1 unit on the horizontal axis to represent 1 book for the x interval 0 to 6, and 1 unit on the vertical axis to represent $10 for the y interval 0 to 90. Do the coordinates of every point on the line make sense for the function? Explain.

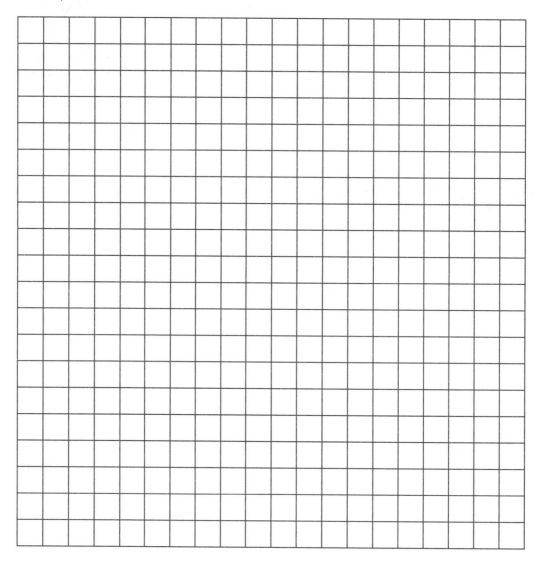

c)   Describe how the slope and y-intercept of the graph are related to the function.

Name: _____   Date: _____

25. At a supermarket, 2 pounds of ham and 3 pounds of turkey are sold for $92.
     Mrs. Field bought 5 pounds of ham and 2 pounds of turkey for $120. Find the
     price of 1 pound of each item.

26. Kenny spends $5 at a toy-capsule vending machine. Every quarter inserted
     into the machine's coin slot dispenses a toy-capsule. The amount of money
     left, A dollars, is a function of the number of toy-capsules dispensed, n.

     a) Write an algebraic equation to represent the function.

     b) Give the least possible input value and the corresponding output value.
         Tell whether the function is increasing or decreasing. Then tell whether the
         function is linear or non-linear. Explain.

     c) Sketch a graph for the function. Identify the y-intercept of the graph.

27. The diagram shows a shelf with braces attached across its backside. The angles made by the braces and the shelf are given as *x* and *y*, as indicated in the diagram. The measure of angle *y* is four times the measure of angle *x*.

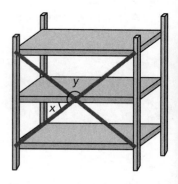

a) Write a system of linear equations for the relationship between the measures of the angles.

b) Graph the two equations on the coordinate plane.

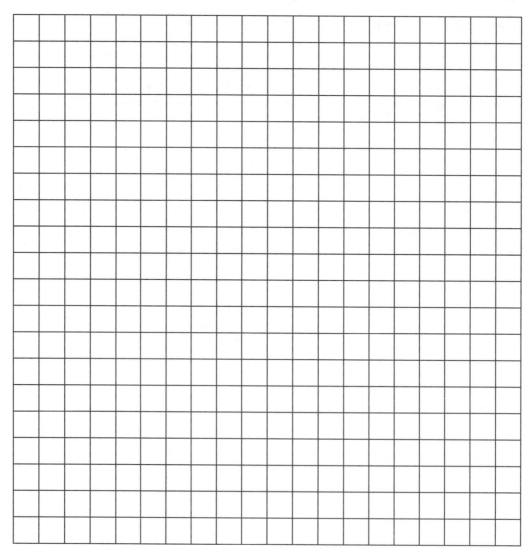

c) Will the measures of the angles ever be the same?

Answers

Chapter 1

Lesson 1.1

1. The base is 5 and the exponent is 2.
2. The base is 8 and the exponent is 4.
3. The base is -3 and the exponent is 8.
4. The base is $\frac{3}{7}$ and the exponent is 9.
5. The base is -2 and the exponent is 4.
6. The base is 1.7 and the exponent is 8.
7. Incorrect. The base is 8 not -8.
8. Correct
9. $6.7 \cdot 6.7 \cdot 6.7 \cdot 6.7 = 6.7^4$
10. $\frac{2}{9} \cdot \frac{2}{9} \cdot \frac{2}{9} = \left(\frac{2}{9}\right)^3$
11. $27 \cdot 27 \cdot 27 \cdot 27 = 27^4$
12. $(-9) \cdot (-9) \cdot (-9) = (-9)^3$
13. $ab \cdot ab \cdot ab \cdot ab = (ab)^4$
14. $w \cdot w \cdot w \cdot w \cdot w \cdot w = w^6$
15. $(-8.8)^3 = (-8.8) \cdot (-8.8) \cdot (-8.8)$
$= -681.472$
16. $3^2 = 3 \cdot 3$
$= 9$
17. $5^3 = 5 \cdot 5 \cdot 5$
$= 125$
18. $\left(\frac{4}{9}\right)^3 = \frac{4}{9} \cdot \frac{4}{9} \cdot \frac{4}{9}$
$= \frac{64}{729}$
19. $1{,}568 = 2 \cdot 784$
$= 2 \cdot 2 \cdot 392$
$= 2 \cdot 2 \cdot 2 \cdot 196$
$= 2 \cdot 2 \cdot 2 \cdot 2 \cdot 98$
$= 2 \cdot 2 \cdot 2 \cdot 2 \cdot 2 \cdot 49$
$= 2 \cdot 2 \cdot 2 \cdot 2 \cdot 2 \cdot 7 \cdot 7$
$= 2^5 \cdot 7^2$
20. $18{,}225 = 3 \cdot 6{,}075$
$= 3 \cdot 3 \cdot 2{,}025$
$= 3 \cdot 3 \cdot 3 \cdot 675$
$= 3 \cdot 3 \cdot 3 \cdot 5 \cdot 135$
$= 3 \cdot 3 \cdot 3 \cdot 5 \cdot 3 \cdot 45$
$= 3 \cdot 3 \cdot 3 \cdot 5 \cdot 3 \cdot 5 \cdot 9$
$= 3 \cdot 3 \cdot 3 \cdot 5 \cdot 3 \cdot 5 \cdot 3 \cdot 3$
$= 3^6 \cdot 5^2$
21. $81 = 3 \cdot 27$
$= 3 \cdot 3 \cdot 9$
$= 3 \cdot 3 \cdot 3 \cdot 3$
$= 3^4$

22. $-8^4 = -4{,}096$, $8^4 = 4{,}096$, $-4^8 = -65{,}536$
$-4^8, -8^4, 8^4$
23. $(-6)^2 = 36$, $(-2)^6 = 64$, $-2^6 = -64$
$-2^6, (-6)^2, (-2)^6$
24. Mars $\approx 10^{22}$ kg, Neptune $\approx 10^{25}$ kg
25. $2 \cdot 2 \cdot 2 \cdot 2 \cdot 2 = 2^5$
26. $128 = 2 \cdot 64$
$= 2 \cdot 2 \cdot 32$
$= 2 \cdot 2 \cdot 2 \cdot 16$
$= 2 \cdot 2 \cdot 2 \cdot 2 \cdot 8$
$= 2 \cdot 2 \cdot 2 \cdot 2 \cdot 2 \cdot 4$
$= 2 \cdot 2 \cdot 2 \cdot 2 \cdot 2 \cdot 2 \cdot 2$
$= 2^7$

The exponent corresponds to the number of folds, so, 7 folds are needed to obtain 128 triangles.

Lesson 1.2

1. $5^8 \cdot 5^2 = 5^{8+2}$
$= 5^{10}$
2. $3.2^4 \cdot 3.2^5 = 3.2^{4+5}$
$= 3.2^9$
3. $\left(\frac{7}{9}\right)^2 \cdot \left(\frac{7}{9}\right)^6 = \left(\frac{7}{9}\right)^{2+6}$
$= \left(\frac{7}{9}\right)^8$
4. $(-12)^8 \cdot (-12) = (-12)^{8+1}$
$= (-12)^9$
5. $q^4 \cdot q^3 = q^{4+3}$
$= q^7$
6. $m^9 \div m^5 = m^{9-5}$
$= m^4$
7. $6xy^2 \cdot 3x^7y^2 = 6 \cdot x \cdot y^2 \cdot 3 \cdot x^7 \cdot y^2$
$= 6 \cdot 3 \cdot x \cdot x^7 \cdot y^2 \cdot y^2$
$= 18 \cdot x^{1+7} \cdot y^{2+2}$
$= 18x^8y^4$
8. $4.5a^3b^7 \cdot 2a^6b = 4.5 \cdot a^3 \cdot b^7 \cdot 2 \cdot a^6 \cdot b$
$= 4.5 \cdot 2 \cdot a^3 \cdot a^6 \cdot b^7 \cdot b$
$= 9 \cdot a^{3+6} \cdot b^{7+1}$
$= 9\,a^9b^8$
9. $(-7)^9 \div (-7)^2 = (-7)^{9-2}$
$= (-7)^7$
10. $\left(\frac{3}{4}\right)^8 \div \left(\frac{3}{4}\right)^5 = \left(\frac{3}{4}\right)^{8-5}$
$= \left(\frac{3}{4}\right)^3$

11. $b^5c^8 \div b^3c^2 = \dfrac{b^5c^8}{b^3c^2}$

$\qquad\qquad\quad = \dfrac{b^5}{b^3} \cdot \dfrac{c^8}{c^2}$

$\qquad\qquad\quad = b^{5-3}c^{8-2}$

$\qquad\qquad\quad = b^2c^6$

12. $72x^9y^7 \div 8x^3y^5 = \dfrac{72x^9y^7}{8x^3y^5}$

$\qquad\qquad\qquad\quad = \dfrac{72}{8} \cdot \dfrac{x^9}{x^3} \cdot \dfrac{y^7}{y^5}$

$\qquad\qquad\qquad\quad = 9x^{9-3}y^{7-5}$

$\qquad\qquad\qquad\quad = 9x^6y^2$

13. $\dfrac{8^9 \cdot 8^2 \cdot 8^6}{8^4 \cdot 8^2 \cdot 8^3} = \dfrac{8^{9+2+6}}{8^{4+2+3}}$

$\qquad\qquad\qquad = \dfrac{8^{17}}{8^9}$

$\qquad\qquad\qquad = 8^{17-9}$

$\qquad\qquad\qquad = 8^8$

14. $\dfrac{\left(\frac{2}{3}\right)^7 \cdot \left(\frac{2}{3}\right)^3 \cdot \left(\frac{2}{3}\right)^9}{\left(\frac{2}{3}\right)^2 \cdot \left(\frac{2}{3}\right)^1 \cdot \left(\frac{2}{3}\right)^4} = \dfrac{\left(\frac{2}{3}\right)^{7+3+9}}{\left(\frac{2}{3}\right)^{2+1+4}}$

$\qquad\qquad\qquad\qquad\qquad = \dfrac{\left(\frac{2}{3}\right)^{19}}{\left(\frac{2}{3}\right)^7}$

$\qquad\qquad\qquad\qquad\qquad = \left(\frac{2}{3}\right)^{19-7}$

$\qquad\qquad\qquad\qquad\qquad = \left(\frac{2}{3}\right)^{12}$

15. $\dfrac{y^3 \cdot y^8 \cdot y^6}{y^4 \cdot y^2 \cdot y^2} = \dfrac{y^{3+8+6}}{y^{4+2+2}}$

$\qquad\qquad\qquad = \dfrac{y^{17}}{y^8}$

$\qquad\qquad\qquad = y^{17-8}$

$\qquad\qquad\qquad = y^9$

16. $\dfrac{5a^5 \cdot 7b^4 \cdot 2b^3}{b^2 \cdot 5b^2 \cdot 2a^4} = \dfrac{5 \cdot 7 \cdot 2 \cdot a^5 \cdot b^4 \cdot b^3}{5 \cdot 2 \cdot b^2 \cdot b^2 \cdot a^4}$

$\qquad\qquad\qquad\qquad = \dfrac{70a^5b^{4+3}}{10b^{2+2}a^4}$

$\qquad\qquad\qquad\qquad = \dfrac{7a^5b^7}{b^4a^4}$

$\qquad\qquad\qquad\qquad = 7(a^{5-4})(b^{7-4})$

$\qquad\qquad\qquad\qquad = 7ab^3$

17. a) $100{,}000 \cdot 100{,}000 \cdot 100{,}000$

$\qquad = 10^5 \cdot 10^5 \cdot 10^5$

$\qquad = 10^{5+5+5}$

$\qquad = 10^{15} \text{ mm}^3$

b) $\dfrac{10^8 \cdot 10^8 \cdot 10^8}{10^{15}} = \dfrac{10^{8+8+8}}{10^{15}}$

$\qquad\qquad\qquad = \dfrac{10^{24}}{10^{15}}$

$\qquad\qquad\qquad = 10^{24-15}$

$\qquad\qquad\qquad = 10^9$

18. Volume of rectangular container
$\qquad = 15p \cdot 12p \cdot 6p$
$\qquad = 1{,}080p^3 \text{ m}^3$

Volume of each cube $= 2p \cdot 2p \cdot 2p$
$\qquad\qquad\qquad\qquad = 8p^3 \text{ m}^3$

Number of cubes that can be packed into

the container $= \dfrac{1{,}080p^3}{8p^3}$

$\qquad\qquad\qquad = 135$

Lesson 1.3

1. $(6^5)^3 = 6^{5 \cdot 3}$
$\qquad\quad = 6^{15}$

2. $(9^6)^4 = 9^{6 \cdot 4}$
$\qquad\quad = 9^{24}$

3. $(34^8)^2 = 34^{8 \cdot 2}$
$\qquad\quad\; = 34^{16}$

4. $(18^6)^7 = 18^{6 \cdot 7}$
$\qquad\quad\; = 18^{42}$

5. $(p^5)^4 = p^{5 \cdot 4}$
$\qquad\quad = p^{20}$

6. $\left[\left(\frac{6}{7}\right)^6\right]^3 = \left(\frac{6}{7}\right)^{6 \cdot 3}$

$\qquad\qquad\quad = \left(\frac{6}{7}\right)^{18}$

7. $[(4b)^4]^4 = (4b)^{4 \cdot 4}$
$\qquad\qquad = (4b)^{16}$

8. $[(28x)^7]^2 = (28x)^{7 \cdot 2}$
$\qquad\qquad\; = (28x)^{14}$

9. $[(-22)^5]^7 = (-22)^{5 \cdot 7}$
$\qquad\qquad\quad = (-22)^{35}$

10. $[(-2q)^4]^2 = (-2q)^{4 \cdot 2}$
$\qquad\qquad\quad = (-2q)^8$

11. $(2^5 \cdot 2^3)^2 = (2^{5+3})^2$
$\qquad\qquad\quad = (2^8)^2$
$\qquad\qquad\quad = 2^{8 \cdot 2}$
$\qquad\qquad\quad = 2^{16}$

12. $(q^7 \cdot q)^4 = (q^{7+1})^4$
$\qquad\qquad\; = (q^8)^4$
$\qquad\qquad\; = q^{8 \cdot 4}$
$\qquad\qquad\; = q^{32}$

13. $\left[\left(\dfrac{5}{6}\right)^3 \cdot \left(\dfrac{5}{6}\right)^2\right]^3 = \left[\left(\dfrac{5}{6}\right)^{3+2}\right]^3$

$\qquad\qquad\qquad = \left[\left(\dfrac{5}{6}\right)^5\right]^3$

$\qquad\qquad\qquad = \left(\dfrac{5}{6}\right)^{5 \cdot 3}$

$\qquad\qquad\qquad = \left(\dfrac{5}{6}\right)^{15}$

14. $\left[\left(-\dfrac{9}{10}\right)^4 \cdot \left(-\dfrac{9}{10}\right)^8\right]^2 = \left[\left(-\dfrac{9}{10}\right)^{4+8}\right]^2$

$\qquad\qquad\qquad\qquad = \left[\left(-\dfrac{9}{10}\right)^{12}\right]^2$

$\qquad\qquad\qquad\qquad = \left(-\dfrac{9}{10}\right)^{12 \cdot 2}$

$\qquad\qquad\qquad\qquad = \left(-\dfrac{9}{10}\right)^{24}$

15. $(2^3 \cdot 2^6)^4 \div 2^8 = (2^{3+6})^4 \div 2^8$

$\qquad\qquad\qquad = (2^9)^4 \div 2^8$

$\qquad\qquad\qquad = 2^{9 \cdot 4} \div 2^8$

$\qquad\qquad\qquad = 2^{36} \div 2^8$

$\qquad\qquad\qquad = 2^{36-8}$

$\qquad\qquad\qquad = 2^{28}$

16. $(11^6 \cdot 11^6)^2 \div 11^9 = (11^{6+6})^2 \div 11^9$

$\qquad\qquad\qquad = (11^{12})^2 \div 11^9$

$\qquad\qquad\qquad = 11^{12 \cdot 2} \div 11^9$

$\qquad\qquad\qquad = 11^{24} \div 11^9$

$\qquad\qquad\qquad = 11^{24-9}$

$\qquad\qquad\qquad = 11^{15}$

17. $(q^7 \cdot q^3)^4 \div q^5 = (q^{7+3})^4 \div q^5$

$\qquad\qquad\qquad = (q^{10})^4 \div q^5$

$\qquad\qquad\qquad = q^{10 \cdot 4} \div q^5$

$\qquad\qquad\qquad = q^{40} \div q^5$

$\qquad\qquad\qquad = q^{40-5}$

$\qquad\qquad\qquad = q^{35}$

18. $(y^9 \cdot y)^3 \div y^{13} = (y^{9+1})^3 \div y^{13}$

$\qquad\qquad\qquad = (y^{10})^3 \div y^{13}$

$\qquad\qquad\qquad = y^{10 \cdot 3} \div y^{13}$

$\qquad\qquad\qquad = y^{30} \div y^{13}$

$\qquad\qquad\qquad = y^{30-13}$

$\qquad\qquad\qquad = y^{17}$

19. $\dfrac{(3^3 \cdot 3^5)^4}{(3^8)^2} = \dfrac{(3^{3+5})^4}{3^{8 \cdot 2}}$

$\qquad\qquad = \dfrac{(3^8)^4}{3^{16}}$

$\qquad\qquad = \dfrac{3^{8 \cdot 4}}{3^{16}}$

$\qquad\qquad = \dfrac{3^{32}}{3^{16}}$

$\qquad\qquad = 3^{32-16}$

$\qquad\qquad = 3^{16}$

20. $\dfrac{(w^9 \cdot w^5)^4}{(w^2)^{11}} = \dfrac{(w^{9+5})^4}{w^{2 \cdot 11}}$

$\qquad\qquad = \dfrac{(w^{14})^4}{w^{22}}$

$\qquad\qquad = \dfrac{w^{14 \cdot 4}}{w^{22}}$

$\qquad\qquad = \dfrac{w^{56}}{w^{22}}$

$\qquad\qquad = w^{56-22}$

$\qquad\qquad = w^{34}$

21. $(u^3 \cdot u^6)^4 \div 8u^2 = (u^{3+6})^4 \div 8u^2$

$\qquad\qquad\qquad = (u^9)^4 \div 8u^2$

$\qquad\qquad\qquad = u^{9 \cdot 4} \div 8u^2$

$\qquad\qquad\qquad = \dfrac{u^{36}}{8u^2}$

$\qquad\qquad\qquad = \dfrac{u^{36-2}}{8}$

$\qquad\qquad\qquad = \dfrac{u^{34}}{8}$

22. $(p^2 \cdot p^5)^9 \div 7p^3 = (p^{2+5})^9 \div 7p^3$

$\qquad\qquad\qquad = (p^7)^9 \div 7p^3$

$\qquad\qquad\qquad = p^{7 \cdot 9} \div 7p^3$

$\qquad\qquad\qquad = \dfrac{p^{63}}{7p^3}$

$\qquad\qquad\qquad = \dfrac{p^{63-3}}{7}$

$\qquad\qquad\qquad = \dfrac{p^{60}}{7}$

23.

$$\frac{\left(\dfrac{3}{7}\right)^5 \cdot \left(\dfrac{9}{7}\right)^2}{\left(\dfrac{3^4}{7^3}\right)^2} = \frac{\left(\dfrac{3}{7}\right)^5 \cdot \left(\dfrac{3^2}{7}\right)^2}{\dfrac{3^{4\cdot2}}{7^{3\cdot2}}}$$

$$= \frac{\left(\dfrac{3}{7}\right)^5 \cdot \left(\dfrac{3^{2\cdot2}}{7^2}\right)}{\dfrac{3^8}{7^6}}$$

$$= \frac{\left(\dfrac{3}{7}\right)^5 \cdot \dfrac{3^4}{7^2}}{\dfrac{3^8}{7^6}}$$

$$= \frac{\dfrac{3^{5+4}}{7^{5+2}}}{\dfrac{3^8}{7^6}}$$

$$= \frac{\dfrac{3^9}{7^7}}{\dfrac{3^8}{7^6}}$$

$$= \frac{3^{9-8}}{7^{7-6}}$$

$$= \frac{3}{7}$$

24.

$$\frac{\left(\dfrac{y}{5}\right)^2 \cdot \left(\dfrac{y^3}{5}\right)^5}{\left(\dfrac{y^2}{5}\right)^6} = \frac{\left(\dfrac{y}{5}\right)^2 \cdot \left(\dfrac{y^{3\cdot5}}{5^5}\right)}{\dfrac{y^{2\cdot6}}{5^{1\cdot6}}}$$

$$= \frac{\left(\dfrac{y}{5}\right)^2 \cdot \left(\dfrac{y^{15}}{5^5}\right)}{\dfrac{y^{12}}{5^6}}$$

$$= \frac{\dfrac{y^2}{5^2} \cdot \dfrac{y^{15}}{5^5}}{\dfrac{y^{12}}{5^6}}$$

$$= \frac{\dfrac{y^{2+15}}{5^{2+5}}}{\dfrac{y^{12}}{5^6}}$$

$$= \frac{\dfrac{y^{17}}{5^7}}{\dfrac{y^{12}}{5^6}}$$

$$= \frac{y^{17-12}}{5^{7-6}}$$

$$= \frac{y^5}{5}$$

Lesson 1.4

1. $7^3 \cdot 4^3 = (7 \cdot 4)^3$
$= 28^3$

2. $8.3^5 \cdot 1.2^5 = (8.3 \cdot 1.2)^5$
$= 9.96^5$

3. $\left(\dfrac{3}{7}\right)^4 \cdot \left(\dfrac{1}{2}\right)^4 = \left(\dfrac{3}{7} \cdot \dfrac{1}{2}\right)^4$
$= \left(\dfrac{3}{14}\right)^4$

4. $\left(-\dfrac{4}{5}\right)^6 \cdot \left(-\dfrac{2}{3}\right)^6 = \left[\left(-\dfrac{4}{5}\right) \cdot \left(-\dfrac{2}{3}\right)\right]^6$
$= \left(\dfrac{8}{15}\right)^6$

5. $p^8 \cdot w^8 = (p \cdot w)^8$
$= (pw)^8$

6. $(5b)^2 \cdot (3c)^2 = (5b \cdot 3c)^2$
$= (15bc)^2$

7. $(6x)^3 \cdot (1.2y)^3 = (6x \cdot 1.2y)^3$
$= (7.2xy)^3$

8. $w^9 \div v^9 = \left(\dfrac{w}{v}\right)^9$

9. $(5c)^5 \div (2b)^5 = \left(\dfrac{5c}{2b}\right)^5$

10. $(8.2y)^4 \div (2x)^4 = \left(\dfrac{8.2y}{2x}\right)^4$
$= \left(\dfrac{4.1y}{x}\right)^4$

11. $21^6 \div 3^6 = \left(\dfrac{21}{3}\right)^6$
$= 7^6$

12. $1.8^3 \div 0.3^3 = \left(\dfrac{1.8}{0.3}\right)^3$
$= 6^3$

13. $9.6^5 \div 3^5 = \left(\dfrac{9.6}{3}\right)^5$
$= 3.2^5$

14. $12^9 \div 21^9 = \left(\dfrac{12}{21}\right)^9$
$= \left(\dfrac{4}{7}\right)^9$

15. $(-20)^2 \div (-5)^2 = \left(\dfrac{-20}{-5}\right)^2$
$= 4^2$

16. $(p^6q^2)^3 = p^{6\cdot3}q^{2\cdot3}$
$= p^{18}q^6$

17. $\left(\dfrac{36b^3}{9a^5}\right)^3 = \dfrac{4^3 b^{3 \cdot 3}}{a^{5 \cdot 3}}$

$\qquad = \dfrac{64b^9}{a^{15}}$

18. $\dfrac{25^2 \cdot 25^6}{5^4 \cdot 5} = \dfrac{25^{2+6}}{5^{4+1}}$

$\qquad = \dfrac{25^8}{5^5}$

$\qquad = \dfrac{(5^2)^8}{5^5}$

$\qquad = \dfrac{5^{2 \cdot 8}}{5^5}$

$\qquad = \dfrac{5^{16}}{5^5}$

$\qquad = 5^{16-5}$

$\qquad = 5^{11}$

19. $\dfrac{8^7 \cdot 8^4 \cdot 2^3}{16^3} = \dfrac{8^{7+4} \cdot 2^3}{(2^4)^3}$

$\qquad = \dfrac{8^{11} \cdot 2^3}{2^{4 \cdot 3}}$

$\qquad = \dfrac{(2^3)^{11} \cdot 2^3}{2^{12}}$

$\qquad = \dfrac{2^{3 \cdot 11} \cdot 2^3}{2^{12}}$

$\qquad = \dfrac{2^{33} \cdot 2^3}{2^{12}}$

$\qquad = \dfrac{2^{33+3}}{2^{12}}$

$\qquad = \dfrac{2^{36}}{2^{12}}$

$\qquad = 2^{36-12}$

$\qquad = 2^{24}$

20. $\dfrac{(9^3)^4 \cdot 6^{12}}{27^{12}} = \dfrac{9^{3 \cdot 4} \cdot 6^{12}}{27^{12}}$

$\qquad = \dfrac{9^{12} \cdot 6^{12}}{27^{12}}$

$\qquad = \left(\dfrac{9 \cdot 6}{27}\right)^{12}$

$\qquad = 2^{12}$

21. $\dfrac{3^6 \cdot (16^3)^2}{12^6} = \dfrac{3^6 \cdot 16^{3 \cdot 2}}{12^6}$

$\qquad = \dfrac{3^6 \cdot 16^6}{12^6}$

$\qquad = \left(\dfrac{3 \cdot 16}{12}\right)^6$

$\qquad = 4^6$

22. $\dfrac{18^8}{6^3 \cdot 3^4 \cdot 6^5} = \dfrac{18^8}{6^{3+5} \cdot 3^4}$

$\qquad = \dfrac{18^8}{6^8 \cdot 3^4}$

$\qquad = \left(\dfrac{18}{6}\right)^8 \left(\dfrac{1}{3^4}\right)$

$\qquad = \dfrac{3^8}{3^4}$

$\qquad = 3^{8-4}$

$\qquad = 3^4$

Lesson 1.5

1. $9^4 \cdot 9^0 = 9^{4+0}$

$\qquad = 9^4$

2. $11^3 \cdot (-11)^0 = 11^3 \cdot 1$

$\qquad = 11^3$

3. $\left(\dfrac{6}{7}\right)^8 \cdot \left(\dfrac{6}{7}\right)^0 = \left(\dfrac{6}{7}\right)^8 \cdot 1$

$\qquad = \left(\dfrac{6}{7}\right)^8$

4. $9^2 \cdot 10^3 + 5^3 \cdot 10^2 + 2^6 \cdot 10^0$
$= 81 \cdot 1{,}000 + 125 \cdot 100 + 64 \cdot 1$
$= 93{,}564$

5. $4.7 \cdot 10^3 + 6 \cdot 10^2 + 7 \cdot 10^0$
$= 4.7 \cdot 1{,}000 + 6 \cdot 100 + 7 \cdot 1$
$= 5{,}307$

6. $\dfrac{5^3 \cdot 5^7}{5^{10}} = \dfrac{5^{3+7}}{5^{10}}$

$\qquad = \dfrac{5^{10}}{5^{10}}$

$\qquad = 1$

7. $(4^{-2})^0 \cdot 7^2 = 1 \cdot 7^2$

$\qquad = 7^2$

$\qquad = 49$

8. $\dfrac{(8^{-4})^{-2} \cdot 7^8}{56^8} = \dfrac{8^{(-4) \cdot (-2)} \cdot 7^8}{56^8}$

$\qquad = \dfrac{8^8 \cdot 7^8}{56^8}$

$\qquad = \dfrac{(8 \cdot 7)^8}{56^8}$

$\qquad = \dfrac{56^8}{56^8}$

$\qquad = 1$

9. $6^{-8} \cdot 6^3 = 6^{-8+3}$

$\qquad = 6^{-5}$

10. $\dfrac{(-9)^{-4}}{(-9)^4} = (-9)^{-4-4}$

$\qquad = (-9)^{-8}$

11. $\dfrac{5}{6} \div \left[\left(\dfrac{5}{6}\right)^7 \cdot \left(\dfrac{5}{6}\right)^0\right] = \dfrac{5}{6} \div \left[\left(\dfrac{5}{6}\right)^7 \cdot 1\right]$

$$= \dfrac{5}{6} \div \left(\dfrac{5}{6}\right)^7$$

$$= \left(\dfrac{5}{6}\right)^{1-7}$$

$$= \left(\dfrac{5}{6}\right)^{-6}$$

12. $\left(\dfrac{3}{8}\right)^{-5} \cdot \left(\dfrac{3}{8}\right)^{-2} \div \left(\dfrac{3}{8}\right)^{-1} = \left(\dfrac{3}{8}\right)^{-5+(-2)} \div \left(\dfrac{3}{8}\right)^{-1}$

$$= \left(\dfrac{3}{8}\right)^{-7} \div \left(\dfrac{3}{8}\right)^{-1}$$

$$= \left(\dfrac{3}{8}\right)^{-7-(-1)}$$

$$= \left(\dfrac{3}{8}\right)^{-6}$$

13. $\dfrac{y^0}{y^4 \cdot y^3} = \dfrac{1}{y^{4+3}}$

$$= \dfrac{1}{y^7}$$

14. $\dfrac{7p^{-6} \cdot 6p^{-3}}{3p^{-5}} = \dfrac{7 \cdot 6 \cdot p^{-6} \cdot p^{-3}}{3p^{-5}}$

$$= \dfrac{42p^{-6+(-3)}}{3p^{-5}}$$

$$= \dfrac{42p^{-9}}{3p^{-5}}$$

$$= 14p^{-9-(-5)}$$

$$= 14p^{-4}$$

15. $4.1^0 \div 3.6^5 = \dfrac{1}{3.6^5}$

16. $9.6^{-4} \div 3.2^{-4} = \left(\dfrac{9.6}{3.2}\right)^{-4}$

$$= 3^{-4}$$

$$= \dfrac{1}{3^4}$$

17. $\dfrac{(-6)^{-8}}{(-6)^3} = (-6)^{-8-3}$

$$= (-6)^{-11}$$

$$= \dfrac{1}{(-6)^{11}}$$

18. $\left(\dfrac{4}{9}\right)^{-7} \cdot \left(\dfrac{4}{9}\right)^{-1} \div \left(\dfrac{4}{9}\right)^{-5} = \left(\dfrac{4}{9}\right)^{-7+(-1)} \div \left(\dfrac{4}{9}\right)^{-5}$

$$= \left(\dfrac{4}{9}\right)^{-8} \div \left(\dfrac{4}{9}\right)^{-5}$$

$$= \left(\dfrac{4}{9}\right)^{-8-(-5)}$$

$$= \left(\dfrac{4}{9}\right)^{-3}$$

$$= \left(\dfrac{9}{4}\right)^3$$

19. $\dfrac{5h^{-2} \cdot 7h^{-4}}{25h^{-9}} = \dfrac{5 \cdot 7 \cdot h^{-2} \cdot h^{-4}}{25h^{-9}}$

$$= \dfrac{35h^{-2+(-4)}}{25h^{-9}}$$

$$= \dfrac{35h^{-6}}{25h^{-9}}$$

$$= \dfrac{7h^{-6-(-9)}}{5}$$

$$= \dfrac{7h^3}{5}$$

20. $\dfrac{b^{16} \cdot b^{-5}}{b^{-7}} = \dfrac{b^{16+(-5)}}{b^{-7}}$

$$= \dfrac{b^{11}}{b^{-7}}$$

$$= b^{11-(-7)}$$

$$= b^{18}$$

21. $\dfrac{4^{-3} \cdot 4^0}{9^4 \cdot 9^{-7}} = \dfrac{4^{-3} \cdot 1}{9^{4+(-7)}}$

$$= \dfrac{4^{-3}}{9^{-3}}$$

$$= \left(\dfrac{4}{9}\right)^{-3}$$

$$= \left(\dfrac{9}{4}\right)^3$$

$$= \dfrac{729}{64}$$

22.
$$\frac{(5^{-2})^4 \cdot 16^{-8}}{40^{-8}} = \frac{5^{(-2)\cdot 4} \cdot 16^{-8}}{40^{-8}}$$
$$= \frac{5^{-8} \cdot 16^{-8}}{40^{-8}}$$
$$= \frac{(5 \cdot 16)^{-8}}{40^{-8}}$$
$$= \frac{80^{-8}}{40^{-8}}$$
$$= \left(\frac{80}{40}\right)^{-8}$$
$$= 2^{-8}$$
$$= \frac{1}{2^8}$$
$$= \frac{1}{256}$$

23.
$$\frac{6^0}{3^{-3} \cdot 2^{-3}} = \frac{1}{(3 \cdot 2)^{-3}}$$
$$= \frac{1}{6^{-3}}$$
$$= 6^3$$
$$= 216$$

24.
$$\frac{\left(5^3\right)^{-4}}{10^{-8} \cdot (-2)^5} = \frac{5^{3 \cdot (-4)}}{10^{-8} \cdot (-2)^5}$$
$$= \frac{5^{-12}}{10^{-8} \cdot (-32)}$$
$$= \frac{5^{-12}}{(2 \cdot 5)^{-8} \cdot (-32)}$$
$$= \frac{5^{-12}}{2^{-8} \cdot 5^{-8} \cdot (-32)}$$
$$= \frac{5^{-12-(-8)}}{2^{-8} \cdot (-32)}$$
$$= \frac{5^{-4}}{2^{-8} \cdot (-32)}$$
$$= -0.0128$$

25.
$$\left(\frac{8v^6}{-64w^0}\right)^{-1} = \left(\frac{8v^6}{-64 \cdot 1}\right)^{-1}$$
$$= \left(-\frac{v^6}{8}\right)^{-1}$$
$$= -\frac{v^{6 \cdot (-1)}}{8^{-1}}$$
$$= -\frac{v^{-6}}{8^{-1}}$$
$$= -\frac{8}{v^6}$$

26.
$$\frac{28x^4y^7}{4x^6y^{-1}} = 7x^{4-6}y^{7-(-1)}$$
$$= 7x^{-2}y^8$$

Lesson 1.6

1. $\sqrt{81} = \sqrt{9^2}$ and $-\sqrt{81} = -\sqrt{9^2}$
  $= 9$ $= -9$

2. $\sqrt{36} = \sqrt{6^2}$ and $-\sqrt{36} = -\sqrt{6^2}$
  $= 6$ $= -6$

3. $\sqrt{97} \approx 9.8$ and $-\sqrt{97} \approx -9.8$

4. $\sqrt{140} \approx 11.8$ and $-\sqrt{140} \approx -11.8$

5. $\sqrt[3]{216} = \sqrt[3]{6^3}$
  $= 6$

6. $\sqrt[3]{343} = \sqrt[3]{7^3}$
  $= 7$

7. $\sqrt[3]{682} \approx 8.8$

8. $\sqrt[3]{\frac{27}{512}} = \sqrt[3]{\frac{3^3}{8^3}}$
  $= \frac{3}{8}$

9. $h^2 = 50.41$
  $\sqrt{h^2} = \sqrt{50.41}$ or $-\sqrt{50.41}$
  $h = 7.1$ or -7.1

10. $d^2 = \frac{49}{81}$
  $\sqrt{d^2} = \sqrt{\frac{7^2}{9^2}}$ or $-\sqrt{\frac{7^2}{9^2}}$
  $d = \frac{7}{9}$ or $-\frac{7}{9}$

11. $a^2 = 144$
  $\sqrt{a^2} = \sqrt{144}$ or $-\sqrt{144}$
  $a = \sqrt{12^2}$ or $-\sqrt{12^2}$
  $a = 12$ or -12

12. $m^2 = 295$
  $\sqrt{m^2} = \sqrt{295}$ or $-\sqrt{295}$
  $m \approx 17.2$ or -17.2

13. $s^3 = 50.653$
  $\sqrt[3]{s^3} = \sqrt[3]{50.653}$
  $s = 3.7$

14. $s^3 = \dfrac{27}{343}$

$\sqrt[3]{s^3} = \sqrt[3]{\dfrac{3^3}{7^3}}$

$s = \dfrac{3}{7}$

15. $s^3 = 2{,}744$

$\sqrt[3]{s^3} = \sqrt[3]{2{,}744}$

$s = 14$

16. $s^3 = 3{,}800$

$\sqrt[3]{s^3} = \sqrt[3]{3{,}800}$

$s \approx 15.6$

17. Let the radius of the lampshade be r inches.

$4\pi r^2 = 57.76\pi$

$\dfrac{1}{4} \cdot 4\pi r^2 = \dfrac{1}{4} \cdot 57.76\pi$

$\pi r^2 = 14.44\pi$

$\dfrac{\pi r^2}{\pi} = \dfrac{14.44\pi}{\pi}$

$r^2 = 14.44$

$\sqrt{r^2} = \sqrt{14.44}$

$r = \sqrt{3.8^2}$

$r = 3.8$ in.

The length of the radius of the lampshade is 3.8 inches.

18. Let the length of each side of the cube be x meters.

$x^3 = 123{,}456$

$\sqrt[3]{x^3} = \sqrt[3]{123{,}456}$

$x \approx 49.8\,\text{m}$

The length of each side of the cube is 49.8 meters.

19. Area of square box $= 2{,}940 \cdot 15$

$\qquad\qquad\qquad = 44{,}100 \text{ cm}^2$

Let the length of each side of the square box be x centimeters.

$x^2 = 44{,}100$

$\sqrt{x^2} = \sqrt{44{,}100}$

$x = 210$ cm

The length of each side of the square box is 210 centimeters.

Brain@Work

1. False. You cannot add terms with different index even though they have the same base.

2. False. You subtract the index for y but not for the coefficients.

3. $a = \dfrac{1}{2}, r = \dfrac{1}{\frac{1}{2}} = \dfrac{2}{1} = \dfrac{4}{2} = 2$

$T_n = ar^{n-1}$ $\qquad\qquad$ $T_n = ar^{n-1}$

$T_{10} = ar^{10-1}$ $\qquad\quad$ $T_{13} = ar^{13-1}$

$T_{10} = \dfrac{1}{2} \cdot 2^9$ $\qquad\quad$ $T_{13} = \dfrac{1}{2} \cdot 2^{12}$

$\quad = 2^{9-1}$ $\qquad\qquad\quad = 2^{12-1}$

$\quad = 2^8$ $\qquad\qquad\qquad = 2^{11}$

Product $= 2^8 \cdot 2^{11}$

$\qquad\quad = 2^{8+11}$

$\qquad\quad = 2^{19}$

$2^8 \div 2^{11} = 2^{8-11}$

$\qquad\qquad = 2^{-3}$

Chapter 2

Lesson 2.1

1. Correct.

2. Incorrect. The coefficient is 21.5. It needs to be less than 10.

3. Correct.

4. Incorrect. The coefficient is less than 1. It needs to be greater than or equal to 1.

5. $6{,}238 = 6.238 \cdot 10^3$

6. $3{,}700{,}000{,}000 = 3.7 \cdot 10^9$

7. $0.00000000000083 = 8.3 \cdot 10^{-13}$

8. $0.0028 = 2.8 \cdot 10^{-3}$

9. $6.05 \cdot 10^1 = 60.5$

10. $8.4 \cdot 10^5 = 840{,}000$

11. $3.82 \cdot 10^{-4} = 0.000382$

12. $9.8 \cdot 10^{-7} = 0.00000098$

13. $10^5 > 10^3$

So, $5.8 \cdot 10^5 > 8.5 \cdot 10^3$.

14. $10^{11} > 10^{10}$

So, $9.6 \cdot 10^{11} > 9.9 \cdot 10^{10}$.

15. $8.8 > 4.8$

So, $8.8 \cdot 10^{-7} > 4.8 \cdot 10^{-7}$.

16. $10^{-3} > 10^{-5}$

So, $1.25 \cdot 10^{-3} > 1.28 \cdot 10^{-5}$.

17.

Fun Facts	Fun Figures in Standard Form	Fun Figures in Scientific Notation
Number of cells in a human body	12,000,000,000,000	$1.2 \cdot 10^{13}$
The diameter of a red blood cell (m)	0.0000084	$8.4 \cdot 10^{-6}$
Average number of times the human eye blinks	4,200,000	$4.2 \cdot 10^{6}$
Number of hairs on a human scalp	100,000	$1 \cdot 10^{5}$
The width of a human hair (cm)	0.00108	$1.08 \cdot 10^{-3}$
Average number of times a human heart beats in its lifetime	3,000 million	$3 \cdot 10^{9}$

18. a)

Airborne Particles	Particle Diameter (m)	Particle Diameter in Scientific Notation (m)
Saw dust	0.000085	$8.5 \cdot 10^{-5}$
Talcum dust	0.00000024	$2.4 \cdot 10^{-7}$
Carbon black dust	0.0000007	$7 \cdot 10^{-7}$
Cement dust	0.000018	$1.8 \cdot 10^{-5}$

  b) Saw dust only. The diameter of saw dust ($8.5 \cdot 10^{-5}$ meter) is greater than the diameter of particles visible to the human eye ($4 \cdot 10^{-5}$ meter).

19. Human eye blink: $3.5 \cdot 10^{5}$ µs
Camera flash: $1,000$ µs $= 1 \cdot 10^{3}$ µs
Camera shutter speed: $4 \cdot 10^{3}$ µs

  a) $1 \cdot 10^{3}$ is the least. So, a camera flash takes the shortest time to complete, which is $1 \cdot 10^{3}$ microseconds.

  b) $3.5 \cdot 10^{5}$ is the greatest.
$3.5 \cdot 10^{5}$ µs
$= 3.5 \cdot 10^{5} \cdot 10^{-6}$ s
$= 3.5 \cdot 10^{5-6}$ s
$= 3.5 \cdot 10^{-1}$ s
So, a human eye blink takes the longest time to complete, which is $3.5 \cdot 10^{-1}$ second.

20. a)

Medium	Speed (m/s)	Speed in Scientific Notation (m/s)
Light	300 million	$3 \cdot 10^{8}$
Sound	330	$3.3 \cdot 10^{2}$

  b) $10^{8} > 10^{2}$
So, the flash of lightning comes first.

Lesson 2.2

1. $7.8 \cdot 10^{5} + 3.9 \cdot 10^{6}$
$= 7.8 \cdot 10^{5} + 39 \cdot 10^{5}$
$= (7.8 + 39) \cdot 10^{5}$
$= 46.8 \cdot 10^{5}$
$= 4.68 \cdot 10^{1} \cdot 10^{5}$
$= 4.68 \cdot 10^{1+5}$
$= 4.68 \cdot 10^{6}$
$\approx 4.7 \cdot 10^{6}$

2. $11.4 \cdot 10^{-3} - 9.8 \cdot 10^{-3}$
$= (11.4 - 9.8) \cdot 10^{-3}$
$= 1.6 \cdot 10^{-3}$

3. $5.6 \cdot 10^{-2} + 8.6 \cdot 10^{-1}$
$= 0.56 \cdot 10^{-1} + 8.6 \cdot 10^{-1}$
$= (0.56 + 8.6) \cdot 10^{-1}$
$= 9.16 \cdot 10^{-1}$
$\approx 9.2 \cdot 10^{-1}$

4. $6.5 \cdot 10^{7} - 2.8 \cdot 10^{6}$
$= 65 \cdot 10^{6} - 2.8 \cdot 10^{6}$
$= (65 - 2.8) \cdot 10^{6}$
$= 62.2 \cdot 10^{6}$
$= 6.22 \cdot 10^{1} \cdot 10^{6}$
$= 6.22 \cdot 10^{1+6}$
$= 6.22 \cdot 10^{7}$
$\approx 6.2 \cdot 10^{7}$

5. a) Total mass of a grain of salt and a grain of sand
$=$ Mass of a grain of salt $+$ Mass of a grain of sand
$= 5.85 \cdot 10^{-5} + 6 \cdot 10^{-4}$
$= 0.585 \cdot 10^{-4} + 6 \cdot 10^{-4}$
$= (0.585 + 6) \cdot 10^{-4}$
$= 6.585 \cdot 10^{-4}$
$\approx 6.6 \cdot 10^{-4}$ g
The total mass of a grain of salt and a grain of sand is approximately $6.6 \cdot 10^{-4}$ gram.

b) Total mass of a grain of rice and a grain of sugar

= Mass of a grain of rice +
  Mass of a grain of sugar

$= 2 \cdot 10^{-2} + 6.5 \cdot 10^{-2}$

$= (2 + 6.5) \cdot 10^{-2}$

$= 8.5 \cdot 10^{-2}$ g

The total mass of a grain of rice and a grain of sugar is approximately $8.5 \cdot 10^{-2}$ gram.

6. Difference in mass between a grain of salt and a grain of sand

= Mass of a grain of sand −
  Mass of a grain of salt

$= 6 \cdot 10^{-4} - 5.85 \cdot 10^{-5}$

$= 6 \cdot 10^{-4} - 0.585 \cdot 10^{-4}$

$= (6 - 0.585) \cdot 10^{-4}$

$= 5.415 \cdot 10^{-4}$

$\approx 5.4 \cdot 10^{-4}$ g

A grain of salt is approximately $5.4 \cdot 10^{-4}$ gram lighter than a grain of sand.

7. Difference in mass between a grain of salt and a grain of rice

= Mass of a grain of rice −
  Mass of a grain of salt

$= 2 \cdot 10^{-2} - 5.85 \cdot 10^{-5}$

$= 2 \cdot 10^{-2} - 0.00585 \cdot 10^{-2}$

$= (2 - 0.00585) \cdot 10^{-2}$

$= 1.99415 \cdot 10^{-2}$

$\approx 2.0 \cdot 10^{-2}$ g

A grain of rice is approximately $2.0 \cdot 10^{-2}$ gram heavier as compared to a grain of salt.

8. a) Driving distance between Phoenix and Los Angeles: 599 km = $5.99 \cdot 10^2$ km
Approximate driving distance between Phoenix and Chicago: $2.3 \cdot 10^3$ km
$10^2 < 10^3$
So, Los Angeles is nearer to Phoenix.

b) Approximate difference in distance traveled

= Approximate driving distance between Phoenix and Chicago −
  Driving distance between Phoenix and Los Angeles

$= 2.3 \cdot 10^3 - 5.99 \cdot 10^2$

$= 23 \cdot 10^2 - 5.99 \cdot 10^2$

$= (23 - 5.99) \cdot 10^2$

$= 17.01 \cdot 10^2$

$= 1.701 \cdot 10^1 \cdot 10^2$

$= 1.701 \cdot 10^{1+2}$

$= 1.701 \cdot 10^3$

$\approx 1.7 \cdot 10^3$ km

So, Andy traveled approximately $1.7 \cdot 10^3$ kilometers farther than Bradley.

9. a) Difference in length of the two ants

= Length of the large ant −
  Length of the small ant

$= 2.5 \cdot 10^{-2} - 2 \cdot 10^{-3}$

$= 2.5 \cdot 10^{-2} - 0.2 \cdot 10^{-2}$

$= (2.5 - 0.2) \cdot 10^{-2}$

$= 2.3 \cdot 10^{-2}$ m

$= 2.3 \cdot 10^{-2} \cdot 10^3$ mm

$= 2.3 \cdot 10^{-2+3}$ mm

$= 2.3 \cdot 10^1$ mm

The large ant is $2.3 \cdot 10^1$ milimeters longer than a small ant.

b) Total length of the trail formed

= Total length of the 2 small ants +
  Length of the large ant

$= 2 \cdot 2 \cdot 10^{-3} + 2.5 \cdot 10^{-2}$

$= 4 \cdot 10^{-3} + 2.5 \cdot 10^{-2}$

$= 0.4 \cdot 10^{-2} + 2.5 \cdot 10^{-2}$

$= (0.4 + 2.5) \cdot 10^{-2}$

$= 2.9 \cdot 10^{-2}$ m

$= 2.9 \cdot 10^{-2} \cdot 10^3$ mm

$= 2.9 \cdot 10^{-2+3}$ mm

$= 2.9 \cdot 10^1$ mm

The total length of the trail formed is $2.9 \cdot 10^1$ milimeters.

Refer to the table below for answers **10 to 13**.

City	Number of Drinking Water Systems (in Scientific Notation)	Population Served (in Scientific Notation)
A	52,873 $= 5.2873 \cdot 10^4$ $\approx 5.3 \cdot 10^4$	300,200,000 $= 3.002 \cdot 10^8$
B	19,400 $= 1.94 \cdot 10^4$ $\approx 1.9 \cdot 10^4$	$6.4 \cdot 10^6$
C	87,672 $= 8.7672 \cdot 10^4$ $\approx 8.8 \cdot 10^4$	13,100,000 $= 1.31 \cdot 10^7$

10. $10^8 > 10^7 > 10^6$
So, city A served the greatest population of 300,200,000, followed by city C with the population of 13,100,000, and city B with the population of $6.4 \cdot 10^6$.

11. City A: Approximately $5.3 \cdot 10^4$;
City B: Approximately $1.9 \cdot 10^4$;
City C: Approximately $8.8 \cdot 10^4$

12. Difference in the population served in city A and city C

= Population served in city A − Population served in city C

= 300,200,000 − 13,100,000

= $3.002 \cdot 10^8 - 1.31 \cdot 10^7$

= $30.02 \cdot 10^7 - 1.31 \cdot 10^7$

= $(30.02 - 1.31) \cdot 10^7$

= $28.71 \cdot 10^7$

= $2.871 \cdot 10^1 \cdot 10^7$

= $2.871 \cdot 10^{1+7}$

= $2.871 \cdot 10^8$

So, the population served in city A is $2.871 \cdot 10^8$ more than the population served in city C.

13. Total population served in the three cities

= Population served in city A + Population served in city B + Population served in city C

= $300,200,000 + 6.4 \cdot 10^6 + 13,100,000$

= $3.002 \cdot 10^8 + 6.4 \cdot 10^6 + 1.31 \cdot 10^7$

= $300.2 \cdot 10^6 + 6.4 \cdot 10^6 + 13.1 \cdot 10^6$

= $(300.2 + 6.4 + 13.1) \cdot 10^6$

= $319.7 \cdot 10^6$

= $3.197 \cdot 10^2 \cdot 10^6$

= $3.197 \cdot 10^{2+6}$

= $3.197 \cdot 10^8$

$\approx 3.2 \cdot 10^8$

So, the total population served in the three cities is approximately $3.2 \cdot 10^8$.

Lesson 2.3

1. $8.5 \cdot 10^{-2} \cdot 9.52 \cdot 10^7$

= $8.5 \cdot 9.52 \cdot 10^{-2} \cdot 10^7$

= $80.92 \cdot 10^{-2} \cdot 10^7$

= $8.092 \cdot 10^1 \cdot 10^{-2} \cdot 10^7$

= $8.092 \cdot 10^{1-2+7}$

= $8.092 \cdot 10^6$

$\approx 8.1 \cdot 10^6$

2. $3.8 \cdot 10^3 \div 4.86 \cdot 10^{-2}$

= $\dfrac{3.8 \cdot 10^3}{4.86 \cdot 10^{-2}}$

= $\dfrac{3.8}{4.86} \cdot \dfrac{10^3}{10^{-2}}$

= $\dfrac{3.8}{4.86} \cdot 10^{3-(-2)}$

= $\dfrac{3.8}{4.86} \cdot 10^{3+2}$

= $\dfrac{3.8}{4.86} \cdot 10^5$

$\approx 7.8 \cdot 10^{-1} \cdot 10^5$

= $7.8 \cdot 10^{-1+5}$

= $7.8 \cdot 10^4$

3. $6.2 \cdot 10^5 \cdot 4.7 \cdot 10^{-8}$

= $6.2 \cdot 4.7 \cdot 10^5 \cdot 10^{-8}$

= $29.14 \cdot 10^5 \cdot 10^{-8}$

= $2.914 \cdot 10^1 \cdot 10^5 \cdot 10^{-8}$

= $2.914 \cdot 10^{1+5-8}$

= $2.914 \cdot 10^{-2}$

$\approx 2.9 \cdot 10^{-2}$

4. $6.8 \cdot 10^{10} \div 2.3 \cdot 10^{-4}$

= $\dfrac{6.8 \cdot 10^{10}}{2.3 \cdot 10^{-4}}$

= $\dfrac{6.8}{2.3} \cdot \dfrac{10^{10}}{10^{-4}}$

= $\dfrac{6.8}{2.3} \cdot 10^{10-(-4)}$

= $\dfrac{6.8}{2.3} \cdot 10^{10+4}$

$\approx 3.0 \cdot 10^{14}$

5. $\dfrac{\text{Length of Mississippi River}}{\text{Length of Colorado River}}$

= $\dfrac{3.860 \cdot 10^3}{8.94 \cdot 10^2}$

= $\dfrac{3.860}{8.94} \cdot \dfrac{10^3}{10^2}$

= $\dfrac{3.86}{8.94} \cdot 10^{3-2}$

= $\dfrac{3.86}{8.94} \cdot 10^1$

= $\dfrac{3.86}{8.94} \cdot 10$

≈ 4.3

The Mississippi River has a length that is approximately 4.3 times as great as the length of Colorado River.

6. $\dfrac{\text{Length of Rio Grande}}{\text{Length of Colorado River}}$

= $\dfrac{1.885 \cdot 10^3}{8.94 \cdot 10^2}$

= $\dfrac{1.885}{8.94} \cdot \dfrac{10^3}{10^2}$

= $\dfrac{1.885}{8.94} \cdot 10^{3-2}$

= $\dfrac{1.885}{8.94} \cdot 10^1$

= $\dfrac{1.885}{8.94} \cdot 10$

≈ 2.1

The Rio Grande has a length that is approximately 2.1 times as great as the length of the Colorado River.

7. $\dfrac{\text{Length of Mississippi River}}{\text{Length of Rio Grande}}$

$= \dfrac{3.86 \cdot 10^3}{1.885 \cdot 10^3}$

$= \dfrac{3.86}{1.885} \cdot 10^{3-3}$

$= \dfrac{3.86}{1.885} \cdot 10^0$

≈ 2.0

The Mississippi River has a length that is approximately 2.0 times as great as the length of the Rio Grande.

8. a) $12\text{ h} = 12 \cdot 60 \cdot 60$

$= 43{,}200$

$= 4.32 \cdot 10^4$ s

Distance

$= \text{Speed} \cdot \text{Time}$

$= 220 \cdot 43{,}200$

$= 2.2 \cdot 10^2 \cdot 4.32 \cdot 10^4$

$= 2.2 \cdot 4.32 \cdot 10^2 \cdot 10^4$

$= 9.504 \cdot 10^2 \cdot 10^4$

$= 9.504 \cdot 10^{2+4}$

$= 9.504 \cdot 10^6$ m

$= 9.504 \cdot 10^6 \cdot 10^{-6}$ m

$= 9.504 \cdot 10^{6-6}$ m

$= 9.504 \cdot 10^0$ m

$= 9.504$ m

The bacteria moved a distance of 9.504 meters.

b) Total distance

$= \text{Number of seconds} \cdot \text{Distance per second}$

$= 5.45 \cdot 10^9 \cdot 8 \cdot 10^{-7}$

$= 5.45 \cdot 8 \cdot 10^9 \cdot 10^{-7}$

$= 43.6 \cdot 10^9 \cdot 10^{-7}$

$= 4.36 \cdot 10^1 \cdot 10^9 \cdot 10^{-7}$

$= 4.36 \cdot 10^{1+9-7}$

$= 4.36 \cdot 10^3$ m

$= 4.36 \cdot 10^3 \cdot 10^6$ μm

$= 4.36 \cdot 10^{3+6}$ μm

$= 4.36 \cdot 10^9$ μm

The bacteria moved a distance of $4.36 \cdot 10^9$ micrometers.

9. Side length of the larger cube:

$8\text{ m} = 8 \cdot 10^2$ cm

Side length of the smaller cube:

$3.5\text{ m} = 3.5 \cdot 10^2$ cm

a) Volume of the large cube before the small cube is cut out

$= 8 \cdot 10^2 \cdot 8 \cdot 10^2 \cdot 8 \cdot 10^2$

$= 8 \cdot 8 \cdot 8 \cdot 10^2 \cdot 10^2 \cdot 10^2$

$= 512 \cdot 10^2 \cdot 10^2 \cdot 10^2$

$= 5.12 \cdot 10^2 \cdot 10^2 \cdot 10^2 \cdot 10^2$

$= 5.12 \cdot 10^{2+2+2+2}$

$= 5.12 \cdot 10^8$ cm^3

b) Volume of the smaller cube

$= 3.5 \cdot 10^2 \cdot 3.5 \cdot 10^2 \cdot 3.5 \cdot 10^2$

$= 3.5 \cdot 3.5 \cdot 3.5 \cdot 10^2 \cdot 10^2 \cdot 10^2$

$= 42.875 \cdot 10^2 \cdot 10^2 \cdot 10^2$

$= 4.2875 \cdot 10^1 \cdot 10^2 \cdot 10^2 \cdot 10^2$

$= 4.2875 \cdot 10^{1+2+2+2}$

$= 4.2875 \cdot 10^7$ cm^3

Volume of the solid left

$= \text{Volume of the large cube} -$
$\quad\text{Volume of the smaller cube}$

$= 5.12 \cdot 10^8 - 4.2875 \cdot 10^7$

$= 51.2 \cdot 10^7 - 4.2875 \cdot 10^7$

$= (51.2 - 4.2875) \cdot 10^7$

$= 46.9125 \cdot 10^7$

$= 4.69125 \cdot 10^1 \cdot 10^7$

$\approx 4.7 \cdot 10^{1+7}$

$= 4.7 \cdot 10^8$ cm^3

10. a) Model A:

$1{,}280 \cdot 720$

$= 1.28 \cdot 10^3 \cdot 7.2 \cdot 10^2$

$= 1.28 \cdot 7.2 \cdot 10^3 \cdot 10^2$

$= 9.216 \cdot 10^3 \cdot 10^2$

$= 0.9216 \cdot 10^1 \cdot 10^3 \cdot 10^2$

$= 0.9216 \cdot 10^{1+3+2}$

$= 0.9216 \cdot 10^6$ p

≈ 0.9 Mp

Model B:

$1{,}024 \cdot 768$

$= 1.024 \cdot 10^3 \cdot 7.68 \cdot 10^2$

$= 1.024 \cdot 7.68 \cdot 10^3 \cdot 10^2$

$= 7.86432 \cdot 10^3 \cdot 10^2$

$= 0.786432 \cdot 10^1 \cdot 10^3 \cdot 10^2$

$= 0.786432 \cdot 10^{1+3+2}$

$= 0.786432 \cdot 10^6$ p

≈ 0.8 Mp

Model C:

$1{,}366 \cdot 768$

$= 1.366 \cdot 10^3 \cdot 7.68 \cdot 10^2$

$= 1.366 \cdot 7.68 \cdot 10^3 \cdot 10^2$

$= 10.49088 \cdot 10^3 \cdot 10^2$

$= 1.049088 \cdot 10^1 \cdot 10^3 \cdot 10^2$

$= 1.049088 \cdot 10^{1+3+2}$

$= 1.049088 \cdot 10^6$ p

≈ 1.0 Mp

Model D:
1,920 · 1,080
$= 1.92 \cdot 10^3 \cdot 1.08 \cdot 10^3$
$= 1.92 \cdot 1.08 \cdot 10^3 \cdot 10^3$
$= 2.0736 \cdot 10^3 \cdot 10^3$
$= 2.0736 \cdot 10^{3+3}$
$= 2.0736 \cdot 10^6 \, p$
$\approx 2.1 \text{ Mp}$

b) $0.9216 < 1$, and $0.786432 < 1$
So, models A and B are not flat screen LCD televisions.

11. a) Time taken for one cycle
$$= \frac{1}{1.5 \cdot 10^9}$$
$$= \frac{1}{1.5} \cdot \frac{10^0}{10^9}$$
$$= \frac{1}{1.5} \cdot 10^{-9} \, s$$
$$\approx 0.67 \text{ ns}$$
So, the CPU takes approximately 0.67 nanosecond to run one cycle.

b) In 1 second, the computer could run $1.5 \cdot 10^9$ cycles and execute $1.7 \cdot 10^9$ instructions.
Average number of cycles per instruction
$$= \frac{1.5 \cdot 10^9}{1.7 \cdot 10^9}$$
$$= \frac{1.5}{1.7} \cdot \frac{10^9}{10^9}$$
$$= \frac{1.5}{1.7}$$
$$\approx 1$$
So, there is approximately 1 cycle per instruction.

12. a) $6 \cdot 10^{-8}$ m
$= 60 \cdot 10^{-1} \cdot 10^{-8}$ m
$= 60 \cdot 10^{-1-8}$ m
$= 60 \cdot 10^{-9}$ m
$= 60$ nm
$2.2 \cdot 10^{-7}$ m
$= 220 \cdot 10^{-2} \cdot 10^{-7}$ m
$= 220 \cdot 10^{-2-7}$ m
$= 220 \cdot 10^{-9}$ m
$= 220$ nm
The approximate diameter is between 60 nanometers and 220 nanometers.

b) 48 nanometers is not in the range of the diameter of a SARS virus. So, it could not be a SARS virus.

13. Distance between towns A and B:
10 Mm $= 10^1 \cdot 10^6$ m
$\qquad = 10^{1+6}$ m
$\qquad = 10^7$ m
Distance between towns A and C:
100 km $= 100 \cdot 10^3$ m
$\qquad = 1 \cdot 10^2 \cdot 10^3$ m
$\qquad = 10^{2+3}$ m
$\qquad = 10^5$ m
$10^5 < 10^7$
So, town C is nearer to town A.

14. Length of organism P:
25 nm $= 25 \cdot 10^{-9}$ m
$\qquad = 2.5 \cdot 10^1 \cdot 10^{-9}$ m
$\qquad = 2.5 \cdot 10^{1-9}$ m
$\qquad = 2.5 \cdot 10^{-8}$ m
Length of organism Q:
2,500 pm $= 2,500 \cdot 10^{-12}$ m
$\qquad = 2.5 \cdot 10^3 \cdot 10^{-12}$ m
$\qquad = 2.5 \cdot 10^{3-12}$ m
$\qquad = 2.5 \cdot 10^{-9}$ m
$10^{-8} > 10^{-9}$
So, organism P has the greater length.

15. Volume of a steel barrel
$= \pi r^2 h$
$\approx 3.14 \cdot \left(\dfrac{22.5}{2}\right)^2 \cdot 33.5 \text{ in}^3$
Volume of oil in 20,000 steel barrels
$\approx 20,000 \cdot 3.14 \cdot \left(\dfrac{22.5}{2}\right)^2 \cdot 33.5$
$= 266,262,187.5$
$\approx 2.7 \cdot 10^8 \text{ in}^3$
There is approximately $2.7 \cdot 10^8$ cubic inches of oil.

Brain@Work

1. 1 trillion $= 10^{12}$
$\qquad = 10^{3+9}$
$\qquad = 10^3 \cdot 10^9$
$\qquad = 1,000 \text{ billion}$
There are 1,000 billions in a trillion.

2. 72,000 trillion $= 7.2 \cdot 10^4 \cdot 10^{12}$
$\qquad = 7.2 \cdot 10^{4+12}$
$\qquad = 7.2 \cdot 10^{16}$

3. Radius of the Earth:
$6{,}300{,}000 \text{ m} = 6.3 \cdot 10^6 \text{ m}$

Volume of the Earth

$= \dfrac{4}{3}\pi r^3$

$\approx \dfrac{4}{3} \cdot 3.14 \cdot (6.3 \cdot 10^6)^3$

$= \dfrac{4}{3} \cdot 3.14 \cdot 6.3^3 \cdot 10^{18}$

$\approx 1{,}050 \cdot 10^{18}$

$= 1.05 \cdot 10^3 \cdot 10^8$

$= 1.05 \cdot 10^{21} \text{ m}^3$

Density of the Earth

$= \dfrac{\text{Mass of the Earth}}{\text{Volume of the Earth}}$

$\approx \dfrac{5.98 \cdot 10^{24}}{1.05 \cdot 10^{21}}$

$= \dfrac{5.98}{1.05} \cdot \dfrac{10^{24}}{10^{21}}$

$\approx 5.7 \cdot 10^{24-21}$

$= 5.7 \cdot 10^3 \text{ kg/m}^3$

So, the density of the Earth is approximately $5.7 \cdot 10^3$ kilograms per cubic meter.

4.

$\sqrt{\dfrac{1.2 \cdot 10^9 \cdot 4.5 \cdot 10^{-4}}{2 \cdot 10^{-2} \cdot 4.8 \cdot 10^{11}}}$

$= \sqrt{\dfrac{1.2 \cdot 4.5 \cdot 10^{9-4}}{2 \cdot 4.8 \cdot 10^{-2+11}}}$

$= \sqrt{\dfrac{5.4 \cdot 10^5}{9.6 \cdot 10^9}}$

$= \sqrt{\dfrac{5.4}{9.6} \cdot 10^{5-9}}$

$= \sqrt{\dfrac{9}{16 \cdot 10^4}}$

$= \dfrac{\sqrt{9}}{\sqrt{16 \cdot 10^4}}$

$= \dfrac{3}{4 \cdot 10^2}$

$= 0.75 \cdot 10^{-2}$

$= 7.5 \cdot 10^{-1} \cdot 10^{-2}$

$= 7.5 \cdot 10^{-1-2}$

$= 7.5 \cdot 10^{-3}$

Cumulative Practice Chapters 1 to 2

1. $30{,}375$
$= 3 \cdot 10{,}125$
$= 3 \cdot 3 \cdot 3{,}375$
$= 3 \cdot 3 \cdot 3 \cdot 1{,}125$
$= 3 \cdot 3 \cdot 3 \cdot 3 \cdot 375$
$= 3 \cdot 3 \cdot 3 \cdot 3 \cdot 3 \cdot 125$
$= 3 \cdot 3 \cdot 3 \cdot 3 \cdot 3 \cdot 5 \cdot 25$
$= 3 \cdot 3 \cdot 3 \cdot 3 \cdot 3 \cdot 5 \cdot 5 \cdot 5$
$= 3^5 \cdot 5^3$

3	30,375
3	10,125
3	3,375
3	1,125
3	375
5	125
5	25
5	5
	1

2. $29{,}400$
$= 2 \cdot 14{,}700$
$= 2 \cdot 2 \cdot 7{,}350$
$= 2 \cdot 2 \cdot 2 \cdot 3{,}675$
$= 2 \cdot 2 \cdot 2 \cdot 3 \cdot 1{,}225$
$= 2 \cdot 2 \cdot 2 \cdot 3 \cdot 5 \cdot 245$
$= 2 \cdot 2 \cdot 2 \cdot 3 \cdot 5 \cdot 5 \cdot 49$
$= 2 \cdot 2 \cdot 2 \cdot 3 \cdot 5 \cdot 5 \cdot 7 \cdot 7$
$= 2^3 \cdot 3 \cdot 5^2 \cdot 7^2$

2	29,400
2	14,700
2	7,350
3	3,675
5	1,225
5	245
7	49
7	7
	1

3. $\dfrac{\left[\left(\frac{3}{7}\right)^2 \cdot \left(\frac{3}{7}\right)^3\right]^3}{\left[\left(\frac{3}{7}\right)^2\right]^3}$

$= \dfrac{\left[\left(\frac{3}{7}\right)^{2+3}\right]^3}{\left(\frac{3}{7}\right)^{2 \cdot 3}}$

$= \dfrac{\left[\left(\frac{3}{7}\right)^5\right]^3}{\left(\frac{3}{7}\right)^6}$

$= \dfrac{\left(\frac{3}{7}\right)^{5 \cdot 3}}{\left(\frac{3}{7}\right)^6}$

$= \dfrac{\left(\frac{3}{7}\right)^{15}}{\left(\frac{3}{7}\right)^6}$

$= \left(\frac{3}{7}\right)^{15-6}$

$= \left(\frac{3}{7}\right)^9$

4. $(m^5 \cdot m^7)^4 \div (3m^2)^3$

$= \dfrac{(m^5 \cdot m^7)^4}{(3m^2)^3}$

$= \dfrac{(m^{5+7})^4}{3^3 \cdot (m^2)^3}$

$= \dfrac{(m^{12})^4}{27 \cdot m^{2 \cdot 3}}$

$= \dfrac{m^{12 \cdot 4}}{27 \cdot m^6}$

$= \dfrac{m^{48}}{27 \cdot m^6}$

$= \dfrac{m^{48-6}}{27}$

$= \dfrac{m^{42}}{27}$

5. $\dfrac{7^4 \cdot 13^4}{(8^0)^4}$

$= \dfrac{(7 \cdot 13)^4}{1^4}$

$= \dfrac{91^4}{1}$

$= 91^4$

6. $\dfrac{4^5 \cdot (-5)^5 \cdot 5^0}{2^{-5}}$

$= \dfrac{[4 \cdot (-5)]^5 \cdot 1}{2^{-5}}$

$= \dfrac{(-20)^5}{2^{-5}}$

$= \dfrac{(-20)^5}{\left(\frac{1}{2^5}\right)}$

$= (-20)^5 \cdot 2^5$

$= [(-20) \cdot 2]^5$

$= (-40)^5$

7. $\left[16^3 \cdot 4^3\right]^4 \div 4^{12}$

$= \dfrac{\left[(16 \cdot 4)^3\right]^4}{4^{12}}$

$= \dfrac{(64)^{3 \cdot 4}}{4^{12}}$

$= \dfrac{64^{12}}{4^{12}}$

$= \left(\dfrac{64}{4}\right)^{12}$

$= 16^{12}$

8. $(81^6 \div 81^3) \cdot \dfrac{(6^0)^3}{3^3 \cdot 9^3}$

$= (81^{6-3}) \cdot \dfrac{1^3}{3^3 \cdot 9^3}$

$= 81^3 \cdot \dfrac{1}{(3 \cdot 9)^3}$

$= \dfrac{81^3}{27^3}$

$= \left(\dfrac{81}{27}\right)^3$

$= 3^3$

9. $12^{-3} \cdot \dfrac{5^0 \cdot 12^{-2}}{4^{-5}}$

$= 12^{-3} \cdot \dfrac{1 \cdot 12^{-2}}{4^{-5}}$

$= \dfrac{12^{-3} \cdot 12^{-2}}{4^{-5}}$

$= \dfrac{12^{-3 + (-2)}}{4^{-5}}$

$= \dfrac{12^{-5}}{4^{-5}}$

$= \left(\dfrac{12}{4}\right)^{-5}$

$= 3^{-5}$

$= \dfrac{1}{3^5}$

10. $8^{-5} \cdot (6^0)^{-5} \cdot \left(\dfrac{1}{2}\right)^{-5} \div 3^{-5}$

$= 8^{-5} \cdot 1^{-5} \cdot \left(\dfrac{1}{2}\right)^{-5} \div 3^{-5}$

$= \dfrac{8^{-5} \cdot 1 \cdot \left(\dfrac{1}{2}\right)^{-5}}{3^{-5}}$

$= \dfrac{\left(8 \cdot \dfrac{1}{2}\right)^{-5}}{3^{-5}}$

$= \dfrac{4^{-5}}{3^{-5}}$

$= \left(\dfrac{4}{3}\right)^{-5}$

$= \dfrac{1}{\left(\dfrac{4}{3}\right)^5}$

$= \dfrac{1}{\left(\dfrac{4^5}{3^5}\right)}$

$= \dfrac{3^5}{4^5}$

$= \left(\dfrac{3}{4}\right)^5$

11. $\sqrt{529} = 23$
or $-\sqrt{529} = -23$

12. $\sqrt{1,056.2} \approx 32.5$
or $-\sqrt{1,056.2} \approx -32.5$

13. $\sqrt[3]{\dfrac{64}{343}} = \sqrt[3]{\left(\dfrac{4}{7}\right)^3}$

$\qquad = \dfrac{4}{7}$

14. $\sqrt[3]{-734.2} \approx -9.0$

15. $2.28 \cdot 10^{12} + 2.69 \cdot 10^{12}$
$\quad = (2.28 + 2.69) \cdot 10^{12}$
$\quad = 4.97 \cdot 10^{12}$
$\quad 8.63 \cdot 10^{12} - 4.09 \cdot 10^{12}$
$\quad = (8.63 - 4.09) \cdot 10^{12}$
$\quad = 4.54 \cdot 10^{12}$
$\quad 4.97 > 4.54$
So, $4.97 \cdot 10^{12} > 4.54 \cdot 10^{12}$

16. $7.4 \cdot 10^{-4} - 6.5 \cdot 10^{-5}$
$\quad = 7.4 \cdot 10^{-4} - 0.65 \cdot 10^1 \cdot 10^{-5}$
$\quad = 7.4 \cdot 10^{-4} - 0.65 \cdot 10^{-4}$
$\quad = (7.4 - 0.65) \cdot 10^{-4}$
$\quad = 6.75 \cdot 10^{-4}$
$\quad 3.6 \cdot 10^{-5} - 7.6 \cdot 10^{-6}$
$\quad = 3.6 \cdot 10^{-5} - 0.76 \cdot 10^1 \cdot 10^{-6}$
$\quad = 3.6 \cdot 10^{-5} - 0.76 \cdot 10^{-5}$
$\quad = (3.6 - 0.76) \cdot 10^{-5}$
$\quad = 2.84 \cdot 10^{-5}$
$\quad 10^{-4} > 10^{-5}$
So, $6.75 \cdot 10^{-4} > 2.84 \cdot 10^{-5}$.

17. $4.8 \cdot 10^8 \cdot 5 \cdot 10^8$
$\quad = 4.8 \cdot 5 \cdot 10^8 \cdot 10^8$
$\quad = 24 \cdot 10^8 \cdot 10^8$
$\quad = 2.4 \cdot 10^1 \cdot 10^8 \cdot 10^8$
$\quad = 2.4 \cdot 10^{1+8+8}$
$\quad = 2.4 \cdot 10^{17}$
$\quad 7.3 \cdot 10^{-6} \cdot 4 \cdot 10^{-3}$
$\quad = 7.3 \cdot 4 \cdot 10^{-6} \cdot 10^{-3}$
$\quad = 29.2 \cdot 10^{-6} \cdot 10^{-3}$
$\quad = 2.92 \cdot 10^1 \cdot 10^{-6} \cdot 10^{-3}$
$\quad = 2.92 \cdot 10^{1+(-6)+(-3)}$
$\quad = 2.92 \cdot 10^{-8}$
$\quad 10^{17} > 10^{-8}$
So, $2.4 \cdot 10^{17} > 2.92 \cdot 10^{-8}$

18. $8.4 \cdot 10^4 \div 7 \cdot 10^6$

$\quad = \dfrac{8.4 \cdot 10^4}{7 \cdot 10^6}$

$\quad = \dfrac{8.4}{7} \cdot \dfrac{10^4}{10^6}$

$\quad = 1.2 \cdot 10^{4-6}$
$\quad = 1.2 \cdot 10^{-2}$
$\quad 7.5 \cdot 10^{-6} \div 1.5 \cdot 10^{-6}$

$\quad = \dfrac{7.5 \cdot 10^{-6}}{1.5 \cdot 10^{-6}}$

$\quad = \dfrac{7.5}{1.5} \cdot \dfrac{10^{-6}}{10^{-6}}$

$\quad = 5 \cdot 10^{-6-(-6)}$
$\quad = 5 \cdot 10^0$
$\quad = 5 \cdot 1$
$\quad = 5$
So, $5 > 1.2 \cdot 10^{-2}$.

19. 0.000000043 meter
= $43 \cdot 10^{-9}$ meter
= 43 nanometers (nm)

20. 0.000093 second
= $93 \cdot 10^{-6}$ second
= 93 microseconds (μs)

21. 42,000,000,000 hertz
= $42 \cdot 10^{9}$ hertz
= 42 gigahertz (GHz)

22. 69,000 bytes
= $69 \cdot 10^{3}$ bytes
= 69 kilobytes (kB)

23. Let the approximate side length of the square base be d meters.
$d^2 \approx 53,065.73$
$d \approx \sqrt{53,065.73}$
   ≈ 230.4
So, the side length of the square base is approximately 230.4 meters.

24. Let the radius of the Moon be r kilometers.
$$\frac{4}{3}\pi r^3 = 2.1958 \cdot 10^{10}$$
$$\frac{3}{4} \cdot \frac{4}{3}\pi r^3 = \frac{3}{4} \cdot 2.1958 \cdot 10^{10}$$
$$\pi r^3 = 1.64685 \cdot 10^{10}$$
$$\frac{\pi r^3}{\pi} = \frac{1.64685 \cdot 10^{10}}{\pi}$$
$$r^3 = \frac{1.64685 \cdot 10^{10}}{3.14}$$
$$r^3 = \frac{16.4685 \cdot 10^{9}}{3.14}$$
$$r = \sqrt[3]{\frac{16.4685}{3.14} \cdot 10^{9}}$$
$$r = \sqrt[3]{\frac{16.4685}{3.14}} \cdot \sqrt[3]{10^{9}}$$
$$r \approx 1.7 \cdot 10^{3}$$
So, the radius of the Moon is approximately $1.7 \cdot 10^{3}$ kilometers.

25. Weight of an empty box:
56.7 g = $56.7 \cdot 10^{-3}$ kg = $5.67 \cdot 10^{-2}$ kg
Total weight of 940 feathers
= $0.000567 \cdot 940$
= $5.67 \cdot 10^{-4} \cdot 9.4 \cdot 10^{2}$
= $5.67 \cdot 9.4 \cdot 10^{-4} \cdot 10^{2}$
= $53.298 \cdot 10^{-4+2}$
= $53.298 \cdot 10^{-2}$
= $5.3298 \cdot 10^{-1}$ kg
Total weight of the box with 940 feathers
= $5.67 \cdot 10^{-2} + 5.3298 \cdot 10^{-1}$
= $0.567 \cdot 10^{1} \cdot 10^{-2} + 5.3298 \cdot 10^{-1}$
= $0.567 \cdot 10^{-1} + 5.3298 \cdot 10^{-1}$
= $(0.567 + 5.3298) \cdot 10^{-1}$
= $5.8968 \cdot 10^{-1}$
$\approx 5.9 \cdot 10^{-1}$ kg
So, the total weight of the box with 940 feathers inside is approximately $5.9 \cdot 10^{-1}$ kilogram.

26. a) Microorganism A:
Speed of movement
= 7 mm/s
= $7 \cdot 10^{-3}$ m/s
Microorganism B:
Speed of movement
= 180 μm/s
= $180 \cdot 10^{-6}$ m/s
= $1.8 \cdot 10^{2} \cdot 10^{-6}$ m/s
= $1.8 \cdot 10^{-4}$ m/s

b) $10^{-4} < 10^{-3}$
$1.8 \cdot 10^{-4} < 7 \cdot 10^{-3}$
So, microorganism B moves at a slower speed.

c) Difference in their speed of movement
= Speed of movement of microorganism A − Speed of movement of microorganism B
= $7 \cdot 10^{-3} - 1.8 \cdot 10^{-4}$
= $7 \cdot 10^{-3} - 0.18 \cdot 10^{1} \cdot 10^{-4}$
= $(7 - 0.18) \cdot 10^{-3}$
= $6.82 \cdot 10^{-3}$
$\approx 6.8 \cdot 10^{-3}$ m/s
So, the difference in the speed of microorganisms A and B speed of approximately is $6.8 \cdot 10^{-3}$ meter per second.

27.

Time (minutes)	Number of Bacteria
1	5
2	$5 \cdot 2^1$
3	$5 \cdot 2 \cdot 2 = 5 \cdot 2^2$
4	$5 \cdot 2^2 \cdot 2 = 5 \cdot 2^3$
n	$5 \cdot 2^{n-1}$

When $n = 15$, number of bacteria
$$= 5 \cdot 2^{15-1}$$
$$= 5 \cdot 2^{14}$$
$$= 81{,}920$$

So, there are 81,920 or $5 \cdot 2^{14}$ bacteria in 15 minutes.

Chapter 3

Lesson 3.1

1.
$$2x + 3(x - 4) = 4(2x + 3)$$
$$2x + 3x - 12 = 8x + 12$$
$$2x + 3x - 8x + 12 = 8x - 8x + 12$$
$$-3x - 12 = 12$$
$$-3x + 12 - 12 = 12 + 12$$
$$-3x = 24$$
$$\frac{-3x}{-3} = \frac{24}{-3}$$
$$x = -8$$

2. $3x + 0.5(10x - 6) = 21$
$$3x + 5x - 3 = 21$$
$$7x - 3 = 21$$
$$8x - 3 + 3 = 21 + 3$$
$$8x = 24$$
$$\frac{8x}{8} = \frac{24}{8}$$
$$x = 3$$

3. $4(x + 2) - 2(x - 4) = 32$
$$4x + 8 - 2x + 8 = 32$$
$$2x + 16 = 32$$
$$2x + 16 - 16 = 32 - 16$$
$$2x = 32$$
$$\frac{2x}{2} = \frac{16}{2}$$
$$x = 8$$

4. $8 - 3(x + 2) = 2(4 - 3x) - 4.5$
$$8 - 3x - 6 = 8 - 6x - 4.5$$
$$2 - 3x = 3.5 - 6x$$
$$2 - 3x + 6x = 3.5 - 6x + 6x$$
$$2 + 3x = 3.5$$
$$2 - 2 + 3x = 3.5 - 2$$
$$3x = 1.5$$
$$x = 0.5$$

5. $0.8(5 + 5x) + 4x = 20$
$$4 + 4x + 4x = 20$$
$$4 + 8x = 20$$
$$4 - 4 + 8x = 20 - 4$$
$$8x = 16$$
$$\frac{8x}{8} = \frac{16}{8}$$
$$x = 2$$

6. $7(x + 5) - 3(2x + 3) = 33.8$
$$7x + 35 - 6x - 9 = 33.8$$
$$x + 26 = 33.8$$
$$x + 26 - 26 = 33.8 - 26$$
$$x = 7.8$$

7. $0.7(3x - 5) + 3.9x = 14.5$
$$2.1x - 3.5 + 3.9x = 14.5$$
$$6x - 3.5 = 14.5$$
$$6x - 3.5 + 3.5 = 14.5 + 3.5$$
$$6x = 18$$
$$\frac{6x}{6} = \frac{18}{6}$$
$$x = 3$$

8.
$$\frac{1}{2}(6x - 8) = \frac{7}{5}(x - 5) - \frac{1}{5}$$
$$\frac{(6x - 8)}{2} = \frac{7(x - 5) - 1}{5}$$
$$10 \cdot \frac{(6x - 8)}{2} = \frac{7x - 35 - 1}{5} \cdot 10$$
$$5(6x - 8) = \frac{7x - 36}{5} \cdot 10$$
$$30x - 40 = 2(7x - 36)$$
$$30x - 40 = 14x - 72$$
$$30x - 40 - 14x = 14x - 72 - 14x$$
$$16x - 40 = -72$$
$$16x - 40 + 40 = -72 + 40$$
$$16x = -32$$
$$\frac{16x}{16} = -\frac{32}{16}$$
$$x = -2$$

9.
$$\frac{x - 4}{10} = \frac{3}{5} - \frac{x - 5}{15}$$
$$\frac{x - 4}{10} = \frac{9 - (x - 5)}{15}$$
$$30 \cdot \frac{x - 4}{10} = \frac{9 - x + 5}{15} \cdot 30$$
$$3(x - 4) = 2(14 - x)$$
$$3x - 12 = 28 - 2x$$
$$3x - 12 + 2x = 28 - 2x + 2x$$
$$5x - 12 + 12 = 28 + 12$$
$$5x = 40$$
$$x = 8$$

10.
$$\frac{1}{6}x = \frac{3x+5}{4} + \frac{1}{3}(x-1)$$
$$\frac{x}{6} = \frac{3x+5}{4} + \frac{(x-1)}{3}$$
$$\frac{2x}{12} = \frac{3(3x+5)+4(x-1)}{12}$$
$$2x = 3(3x+5)+4(x-1)$$
$$2x = 9x+15+4x-4$$
$$2x = 13x+11$$
$$2x-13x = 13x+11-13x$$
$$-11x = 11$$
$$\frac{-11x}{-11} = \frac{11}{-11}$$
$$x = -1$$

11.
$$\frac{2(2x+1)}{5} - \frac{x+2}{3} = \frac{1}{5}$$
$$\frac{4x+2}{5} - \frac{x+2}{3} = \frac{1}{5}$$
$$\frac{3(4x+2)-5(x+2)}{15} = \frac{3}{15}$$
$$\frac{12x+6-5x-10}{15} = \frac{3}{15}$$
$$\frac{7x-4}{15} = \frac{3}{15}$$
$$7x-4 = 3$$
$$7x-4+4 = 3+4$$
$$7x = 7$$
$$\frac{7x}{7} = \frac{7}{7}$$
$$x = 1$$

12.
$$\frac{x+3}{2} - \frac{11-x}{5} = 1 + \frac{3x-1}{20}$$
$$\frac{10(x+3)-4(11-x)}{20} = \frac{20+(3x-1)}{20}$$
$$10x+30-44+4x = 20+3x-1$$
$$14x-14 = 3x+19$$
$$14x-14+14 = 3x+19+14$$
$$14x = 3x+33$$
$$14x-3x = 3x+33-3x$$
$$11x = 33$$
$$\frac{11x}{11} = \frac{33}{11}$$
$$x = 3$$

13. $0.\overline{4}$
Let $x = 0.\overline{4}$; $x = 0.4444444...$ and
$10x = 4.4444444...$
$10x - x = 4.\overline{4} - 0.\overline{4}$
$9x = 4$
$\frac{9x}{9} = \frac{4}{9}$

$x = \frac{4}{9}$

14. $0.0\overline{3}$
Let $x = 0.0\overline{3}$; $x = 0.0333333...$ and
$10x = 0.3333333...$
$10x - x = 0.\overline{3} - 0.0\overline{3}$
$9x = 0.3$
$\frac{9x}{9} = \frac{0.3}{9}$
$x = \frac{1}{30}$

15. $0.1\overline{5}$
Let $x = 0.1\overline{5}$; $x = 0.1555555...$ and
$10x = 1.5555555...$
$10x - x = 1.\overline{5} - 0.1\overline{5}$
$9x = 1.4$
$\frac{9x}{9} = \frac{1.4}{9}$
$x = \frac{7}{45}$

16. $0.2\overline{5}$
Let $x = 0.2\overline{5}$; $x = 0.2555555...$ and
$10x = 2.5555555...$
$10x - x = 2.\overline{5} - 0.2\overline{5}$
$9x = 2.3$
$\frac{9x}{9} = \frac{2.3}{9}$
$x = \frac{23}{90}$

17. $0.41\overline{6}$
Let $x = 0.41\overline{6}$; $x = 0.4166666...$ and
$10x = 4.1666666...$
$10x - x = 4.1\overline{6} - 0.41\overline{6}$
$9x = 3.75$
$\frac{9x}{9} = \frac{3.75}{9}$
$x = \frac{5}{12}$

18. $0.3\overline{18}$
Let $x = 0.3\overline{18}$; $x = 0.3181818...$ and
$100x = 31.8181818...$
$100x - x = 3\overline{1.8} - 0.3\overline{18}$
$99x = 31.5$
$\frac{99x}{99} = \frac{31.5}{99}$
$x = \frac{7}{22}$

19. Let the number of dimes she used be x.
Number of quarters she used
$= x - 5$
$\$2.95 = 295$ cents
$10x + 25(x - 5) = 295$
$10x + 25x - 125 = 295$
$35x - 125 + 125 = 295 + 125$
$$35x = 420$$
$$\frac{35x}{35} = \frac{420}{35}$$
$$x = 12$$
$x - 5 = 12 - 5$
$\qquad = 7$
She used 12 dimes and 7 quarters to pay for the granola bar.

20. Let the price per pound for the ground turkey be x dollars.
$$3\tfrac{1}{2} \cdot x + 2\tfrac{1}{2}(x - 4.60) = 51.50$$
$$6x - 11.50 = 51.50$$
$$6x - 11.50 + 11.50 = 51.50 + 11.50$$
$$6x = 63$$
$$\frac{6x}{6} = \frac{63}{6}$$
$$x = 10.50$$
Price per pound for the white fish
$= \$10.50 - \$4.60$
$= \$5.90$
The price per pound for the white fish is $\$5.90$.

21. Let the weight of bag A be x pounds.
Weight of bag B $= (3 + 2x)$ lb
Weight of bag A + Weight of bag B $= 27$
$$x + 3 + 2x = 27$$
$$3x + 3 = 27$$
$$3x + 3 - 3 = 27 - 3$$
$$3x = 24$$
$$\frac{3x}{3} = \frac{24}{3}$$
$$x = 8$$
The weight of bag A is 8 pounds.

Weight of bag B $= 3 + 2x$; Substitute $x = 8$
$\qquad = 3 + 2(8)$
$\qquad = 19$
The weight of bag B is 19 pounds.

22. Let Gary's age be x.
Two years ago: Gary's age was $x - 2$; and Gary's grandfather's age was $3(x - 2)$

a) If their age difference is 48 years, then
$3(x - 2) - (x - 2) = 48$.

b) Solve for x first:
$$3(x - 2) - (x - 2) = 48$$
$$3x - 6 - x + 2 = 48$$
$$2x - 4 = 48$$
$$2x - 4 + 4 = 48 + 4$$
$$2x = 52$$
$$\frac{2x}{2} = \frac{52}{2}$$
$$x = 26$$
Substitute $x = 26$ into $3(x - 2) + 2$ to find Gary's grandfather's age:
$$3(x - 2) + 2 = 3(26 - 2) + 2$$
$$= 78 - 6 + 2$$
$$= 74$$
Today Gary's grandfather is 74 years old.

23. a) Let x be the number of female students in the class.
Then the number of male students $= 40 - x$
Number of counters given to female students $= 5x$
Number of counters given to male students $= 3(40 - x)$
So, $5x - 3(40 - x) = 128$.
$$5x - 3(40 - x) = 128$$
$$5x - 120 + 3x = 128$$
$$8x - 120 = 128$$
$$8x - 120 + 120 = 128 + 120$$
$$8x = 248$$
$$\frac{8x}{8} = \frac{248}{8}$$
$$x = 31$$
There are 31 female students in the class.

24. a) Let the length of pole A be x.
Length of pole B $= 1\tfrac{3}{4}x$

Length of pole C $= x + 2\tfrac{1}{2}$

Total combined length of 3 poles:
$$47\tfrac{1}{2} = x + 1\tfrac{3}{4}x + (x + 2\tfrac{1}{2})$$

b) Solve to find the length of pole C

$$x + 1\frac{3}{4}x + (x + 2\frac{1}{2}) = 47\frac{1}{2}$$

$$x + 1\frac{3}{4}x + x + 2\frac{1}{2} = 47\frac{1}{2}$$

$$\frac{15}{4}x + 2\frac{1}{2} = 47\frac{1}{2}$$

$$\frac{15}{4}x + 2\frac{1}{2} - 2\frac{1}{2} = 47\frac{1}{2} - 2\frac{1}{2}$$

$$\frac{15}{4}x = 45$$

$$\frac{4}{15} \cdot \frac{15}{4}x = 45 \cdot \frac{4}{15}$$

$$x = 12$$

The length of pole C $= x + 2\frac{1}{2}$

$$= 12 + 2\frac{1}{2}$$

$$= 14\frac{1}{2}$$

The length of pole C is $14\frac{1}{2}$ inches.

Lesson 3.2

1.
$$\frac{4}{5}x + 18 = -2(3 + 2x)$$

$$\frac{4}{5}x + 18 = -6 - 4x$$

$$\frac{4}{5}x + 18 - 18 = -6 - 4x - 18$$

$$\frac{4}{5}x = -24 - 4x$$

$$\frac{4}{5}x + 4x = -24 - 4x + 4x$$

$$\frac{24}{5}x = -24$$

$$\frac{5}{24} \cdot \frac{24}{5}x = -24 \cdot \frac{5}{24}$$

$$x = -5$$

One solution

2. $7 + 2(x - 6) = -3 + 2(x - 1)$
$7 + 2x - 12 = -3 + 2x - 2$
$2x - 5 = 2x - 5$
$2x - 5 + 5 = 2x - 5 + 5$
$2x = 2x$
$\frac{2x}{2} = \frac{2x}{2}$
$x = x$
Infinite solutions

3. $2(4 - \frac{1}{3}x) = x + 3(x - 2)$

$$8 - \frac{2}{3}x = x + 3x - 6$$

$$8 - \frac{2}{3}x = 4x - 6$$

$$8 - 8 - \frac{2}{3}x = 4x - 6 - 8$$

$$-\frac{2}{3}x = 4x - 14$$

$$-\frac{2}{3}x - 4x = 4x - 4x - 14$$

$$-\frac{14}{3}x = -14$$

$$-\frac{3}{14} \cdot (-\frac{14}{3}x) = -14 \cdot (-\frac{3}{14})$$

$$x = 3$$

One solution

4. $\frac{2}{5}(1 - 5x) = -\frac{1}{2}(4x + 3)$

$$\frac{2}{5} - 2x = -2x - \frac{3}{2}$$

$$\frac{2}{5} - 2x + 2x = -2x - \frac{3}{2} + 2x$$

$$\frac{2}{5} \neq -\frac{3}{2}$$

No solution

5. $5(5 - 2x) - 6(2 - x) = 7(1 - x)$
$25 - 10x - 12 + 6x = 7 - 7x$
$13 - 4x = 7 - 7x$
$13 - 4x + 7x = 7 - 7x + 7x$
$13 + 3x = 7$
$13 - 13 + 3x = 7 - 13$
$3x = -6$
$x = -2$
One solution

6. $0.5(3x + 5) - 0.1(12x - 5) = 3(1 + 0.1x)$
$1.5x + 2.5 - 1.2x + 0.5 = 3 + 0.3x$
$0.3x + 3 = 3 + 0.3x$
$0.3x - 0.3x + 3 = 3 + 0.3x - 0.3x$
$3 = 3$
Infinite solutions

7. $4(2 - x) + 2(1 - 5x) = 5(2 - 3x) + x$
$8 - 4x + 2 - 10x = 10 - 15x + x$
$10 - 14x = 10 - 14x$
$10 + 14x - 14x = 10 - 14x + 14x$
$10 = 10$
Infinite solutions

8. $3(\frac{2}{9}x - 1) = 1 - \frac{2}{3}(x + 1) + \frac{4}{3}x$

$$\frac{2}{3}x - 3 = 1 - \frac{2}{3}x - \frac{2}{3} + \frac{4}{3}x$$

$$\frac{2}{3}x - 3 = \frac{1}{3} + \frac{2}{3}x$$

$$\frac{2}{3}x - \frac{2}{3}x - 3 = \frac{1}{3} + \frac{2}{3}x - \frac{2}{3}x$$

$$-3 \neq \frac{1}{3}$$

No solution

9. $2(x + 5) - 2 = 1.5(10 - x)$
$2x + 10 - 2 = 15 - 1.5x$
$2x + 8 = 15 - 1.5x$
$2x + 8 + 1.5x = 15 - 1.5x + 1.5x$
$3.5x + 8 = 15$
$3.5x + 8 - 8 = 15 - 8$
$3.5x = 7$
$$\frac{3.5x}{3.5} = \frac{7}{3.5}$$
$x = 2$

One solution

10. $2(x - 3) + \frac{1}{2}(7 + 2x) = \frac{1}{2} + 3(x - 1)$

$$2x - 6 + \frac{7}{2} + x = \frac{1}{2} + 3x - 3$$

$$3x - \frac{5}{2} = -\frac{5}{2} + 3x$$

$$3x - \frac{5}{2} + \frac{5}{2} = -\frac{5}{2} + 3x + \frac{5}{2}$$

$$3x = 3x$$

$$\frac{3x}{3} = \frac{3x}{3}$$

$$x = x$$

Infinite solutions

11. a) Height of stool Y
$= (h + 5.5)$ in.
Height of stool Z
$= (h + 13)$ in.

b) $2Z = X + Y$
$2(h + 13) = h + (h + 5.5)$
$2h + 26 = 2h + 5.5$
$2h - 2h + 26 = 2h - 2h + 5.5$
$26 \neq 5.5$

Since there is no solution to this equation, you cannot solve for the height of stool x.

12. If the triangle is an isosceles triangle, then
$AB = AC$

$$6(3 - \frac{1}{4}x) = (\frac{3}{4}x + 5 - 2\frac{1}{4}x)$$

$$18 - \frac{3}{2}x = -\frac{3}{2}x + 5$$

$$18 - \frac{3}{2}x + \frac{3}{2}x = -\frac{3}{2}x + \frac{3}{2}x - 5$$

$$18 \neq -5$$

Since there is no solution to the equation, you cannot determine if $AB = AC$. So you cannot determine that triangle ABC is an isosceles triangle.

Lesson 3.3

1. $m = 1,000k$

2. $u = 16p$

3. $h = 24d$

4. $b = 10^6 m$

5. $4 - 2x = 8 + y$
$4 - 2(-3) = 8 + y$
$10 = 8 + y$
$10 - 8 = 8 + y - 8$
$2 = y$

6. $y = \frac{5}{4}(x + 7)$

$$y = \frac{5}{4}(-3 + 7)$$

$$y = 5$$

7. $3(y - 5) = 5x + 3$
$3y - 15 = 5(-3) + 3$
$3y - 15 = -12$
$3y - 15 + 15 = -12 + 15$
$3y = 3$
$$\frac{3y}{3} = \frac{3}{3}$$
$y = 1$

8. $7(x - 3) = 6y$
$7(-3 - 3) = 6y$
$-42 = 6y$
$$\frac{-42}{6} = \frac{6y}{6}$$
$-7 = y$

9. $3(x - 3) = 2y$
$3x - 9 = 2(5)$
$3x - 9 = 10$
$3x - 9 + 9 = 10 + 9$
$3x = 19$
$$\frac{3x}{3} = \frac{19}{3}$$
$$x = 6\frac{1}{3}$$

10.
$$\frac{5x - 3}{2} = 2(y + 3)$$
$$\frac{5x}{2} - \frac{3}{2} = 2(5 + 3)$$
$$\frac{5x}{2} - \frac{3}{2} = 16$$
$$\frac{5x}{2} - \frac{3}{2} + \frac{3}{2} = 16 + \frac{3}{2}$$
$$\frac{5x}{2} = \frac{35}{2}$$
$$\frac{2}{5} \cdot \frac{5x}{2} = \frac{35}{2} \cdot \frac{2}{5}$$
$$x = 7$$

11.
$$3x + 2y = 0.2(2y + 1)$$
$$3x + 2y = 0.4y + 0.2$$
$$3x + 2(5) = 0.4(5) + 0.2$$
$$3x + 10 = 2.0 + 0.2$$
$$3x + 10 = 2.2$$
$$3x + 10 - 10 = 2.2 - 10$$
$$3x = -7.8$$
$$\frac{3x}{3} = -\frac{7.8}{3}$$
$$x = -2.6$$

12.
$$7y - 4x = 51$$
$$7(5) - 4x = 51$$
$$35 - 4x = 51$$
$$35 - 35 - 4x = 51 - 35$$
$$-4x = 16$$
$$\frac{-4x}{-4} = \frac{16}{-4}$$
$$x = -4$$

13. $y = \frac{1}{3}(9x - 18)$

Substitute $x = 2$ into the equation
$$y = \frac{1}{3}[9(2) - 18]$$
$$y = \frac{1}{3}(0)$$
$$y = 0$$
Substitute $x = 3$ into the equation
$$y = \frac{1}{3}[9(3) - 18]$$
$$y = \frac{1}{3}(9)$$
$$y = 3$$
Substitute $x = 4$ into the equation
$$y = \frac{1}{3}[9(4) - 18]$$
$$y = \frac{1}{3}(18)$$
$$y = 6$$

So the table of values is:

x	2	3	4
y	0	3	6

14. $3x - 4 = \frac{1}{5}(y - 5)$

Substitute $x = 2$ into the equation
$$3(2) - 4 = \frac{1}{5}(y - 5)$$
$$6 - 4 = \frac{y}{5} - 1$$
$$2 = \frac{y}{5} - 1$$
$$2 + 1 = \frac{y}{5} - 1 + 1$$
$$3 = \frac{y}{5}$$
$$5 \cdot 3 = \frac{y}{5} \cdot 5$$
$$y = 15$$
Substitute $x = 3$ into the equation
$$3(3) - 4 = \frac{1}{5}(y - 5)$$
$$9 - 4 = \frac{y}{5} - 1$$
$$5 = \frac{y}{5} - 1$$
$$5 + 1 = \frac{y}{5} - 1 + 1$$
$$6 = \frac{y}{5}$$
$$5 \cdot 6 = \frac{y}{5} \cdot 5$$
$$y = 30$$
Substitute $x = 4$ into the equation
$$3(4) - 4 = \frac{1}{5}(y - 5)$$
$$12 - 4 = \frac{y}{5} - 1$$
$$8 = \frac{y}{5} - 1$$
$$8 + 1 = \frac{y}{5} - 1 + 1$$
$$9 = \frac{y}{5}$$
$$5 \cdot 9 = \frac{y}{5} \cdot 5$$
$$y = 45$$

So the table of values is:

x	2	3	4
y	15	30	45

15. $-7y = 4x - 3$

Substitute $x = 2$ into the equation
$-7y = 4(2) - 3$
$-7y = 5$
$\dfrac{-7y}{-7} = \dfrac{5}{-7}$
$y = -\dfrac{5}{7}$

Substitute $x = 3$ into the equation
$-7y = 4(3) - 3$
$-7y = 9$
$\dfrac{-7y}{-7} = \dfrac{9}{-7}$
$y = -1\dfrac{2}{7}$

Substitute $x = 4$ into the equation
$-7y = 4(4) - 3$
$-7y = 13$
$\dfrac{-7y}{-7} = \dfrac{13}{-7}$
$y = -1\dfrac{6}{7}$

So the table of values is:

x	2	3	4
y	$-\dfrac{5}{7}$	$-1\dfrac{2}{7}$	$-1\dfrac{6}{7}$

16. $\dfrac{1}{4}(6x + 1) = \dfrac{1}{2}(y + 2)$

Substitute $x = 2$ into the equation
$\dfrac{1}{4}[6(2) + 1] = \dfrac{1}{2}(y + 2)$
$\dfrac{13}{4} = \dfrac{y}{2} + 1$
$\dfrac{13}{4} - 1 = \dfrac{y}{2} + 1 - 1$
$\dfrac{9}{2} = \dfrac{y}{2}$
$2 \cdot \dfrac{9}{4} = \dfrac{y}{2} \cdot 2$
$4\dfrac{1}{2} = y$

Substitute $x = 3$ into the equation
$\dfrac{1}{4}[6(3) + 1] = \dfrac{1}{2}(y + 2)$
$\dfrac{19}{4} = \dfrac{y}{2} + 1$
$\dfrac{19}{4} - 1 = \dfrac{y}{2} + 1 - 1$
$2 \cdot \dfrac{15}{4} = \dfrac{y}{2} \cdot 2$
$7\dfrac{1}{2} = y$

Substitute $x = 4$ into the equation
$\dfrac{1}{4}[6(4) + 1] = \dfrac{1}{2}(y + 2)$
$\dfrac{25}{4} = \dfrac{y}{2} + 1$
$\dfrac{25}{4} - 1 = \dfrac{y}{2} + 1 - 1$
$2 \cdot \dfrac{21}{4} = \dfrac{y}{2} \cdot 2$
$10\dfrac{1}{2} = y$

So the table of values is:

x	2	3	4
y	$4\dfrac{1}{2}$	$7\dfrac{1}{2}$	$10\dfrac{1}{2}$

17. $y = 4(2x + 1)$

Substitute $x = 1$ into the equation
$y = 4[2(1) + 1]$
$y = 12$
Substitute $x = 2$ into the equation
$y = 4[2(2) + 1]$
$y = 20$
Substitute $x = 3$ into the equation
$y = 4[2(3) + 1]$
$y = 28$

x	1	2	3
y	12	20	28

18. $x + \dfrac{y}{3} = 2$

Substitute $y = 9$ into the equation
$x + \dfrac{9}{3} = 2$
$x + 3 = 2$
$x + 3 - 3 = 2 - 3$
$x = -1$

Substitute $y = 3$ into the equation
$x + \dfrac{3}{3} = 2$
$x + 1 = 2$
$x + 1 - 1 = 2 - 1$
$x = 1$

Substitute $x = 3$ into the equation
$3 + \dfrac{y}{3} = 2$
$3 - 3 + \dfrac{y}{3} = 2 - 3$
$\dfrac{y}{3} = -1$
$3 \cdot \dfrac{y}{3} = -1 \cdot 3$

$y = -3$

x	−1	1	3
y	9	3	−3

19. $4(y - 3x) = \dfrac{4}{5}$

Substitute $y = \dfrac{1}{5}$ into the equation

$$4\left[\left(\frac{1}{5}\right) - 3x\right] = \frac{4}{5}$$

$$\frac{4}{5} - 12x = \frac{4}{5}$$

$$\frac{4}{5} - \frac{4}{5} - 12x = \frac{4}{5} - \frac{4}{5}$$

$$-12x = 0$$

$$\frac{-12x}{-12} = \frac{0}{-12}$$

$$x = 0$$

Substitute $x = 1$ into the equation

$$4\left[y - 3(1)\right] = \frac{4}{5}$$

$$4y - 12 = \frac{4}{5}$$

$$4y - 12 + 12 = \frac{4}{5} + 12$$

$$4y = \frac{64}{5}$$

$$\frac{1}{4} \cdot 4y = \frac{64}{5} \cdot \frac{1}{4}$$

$$y = 3\frac{1}{5}$$

Substitute $x = 2$ into the equation

$$4\left[y - 3(2)\right] = \frac{4}{5}$$

$$4y - 24 = \frac{4}{5}$$

$$4y - 24 + 24 = \frac{4}{5} + 24$$

$$4y = \frac{124}{5}$$

$$\frac{1}{4} \cdot 4y = \frac{124}{5} \cdot \frac{1}{4}$$

$$y = 6\frac{1}{5}$$

x	0	1	2
y	$\frac{1}{5}$	$3\frac{1}{5}$	$6\frac{1}{5}$

20. $3x = 5(y - 7)$

Substitute $y = -5$ into the equation

$3x = 5[(-5) - 7)]$

$3x = -60$

$\dfrac{3x}{3} = -\dfrac{60}{3}$

$x = -20$

Substitute $y = 10$ into the equation

$3x = 5[(10) - 7)]$

$3x = 15$

$\dfrac{3x}{3} = \dfrac{15}{3}$

$x = 5$

Substitute $y = 25$ into the equation

$3x = 5[(25) - 7)]$

$3x = 90$

$\dfrac{3x}{3} = \dfrac{90}{3}$

$x = 30$

x	−20	5	30
y	−5	10	25

21. a) $C = 2n - 1$

b) When $n = 30$, $C = 2(30) - 1$

$\qquad\qquad\qquad\quad = 59$

The cost of the 30 rolls was $59.

22. a) $W = 50 + 2t$

b)

Time (t minutes)	20	40	60	80
Amount of water in (W tank litres)	90	130	170	210

c) Substitute $t = 300$ into the equation.

$W = 50 + 2t$

$= 50 + 2(300)$

$= 650$

After 5 hours, there is 650 liters of water in the tank.

d) $W = 50 + 2t$

$1,000 = 50 + 2t$

$2t = 950$

$t = 475$ minutes; 7 hours 55 minutes

It will take 7 hours and 55 minutes to completely fill the tank.

23. a) $A = 40 + 7.5t$

b)

Amount in Bank (A dollars)	70	85	100
Time Worked (t weeks)	4	6	8

c)
$$A = 40 + 7.5t$$
$$175 = 40 + 7.5t$$
$$175 - 40 + 7.5t - 40$$
$$135 = 7.5t$$
$$\frac{135}{7.5} = \frac{7.5t}{7.5}$$
$$18 = t$$
In 18 weeks, Joel will have enough money for his season pass.

24. a) $M = 90 + \frac{1}{4}n$

M	106	109	112	115
n	64	76	88	100

b) $M = 90 + \frac{1}{4}n$
$$= 90 + \frac{1}{4}(360)$$
$$= 90 + 90$$
$$= 180$$
Annabel's weekly pay was $180.

c)
$$M = 90 + \frac{1}{4}n$$
$$130 = 90 + \frac{1}{4}n$$
$$130 - 90 = 90 - 90 + \frac{1}{4}n$$
$$40 = \frac{1}{4}n$$
$$4 \cdot 40 = \frac{1}{4}n \cdot 4$$
$$160 = n$$
Annabel sold 160 tubes of sunscreen that week.

Lesson 3.4

1.
$$2(x + 1) = 7 - y$$
$$2x + 2 = 7 - y$$
$$2x + 2 - 2 = 7 - y - 2$$
$$2x = 5 - y$$
$$y = 5 - 2x$$

When $x = -2$
$$y = 5 - 2(-2)$$
$$y = 9$$

2.
$$4 - 2y = 5x - 3$$
$$4 - 5x = 2y - 3$$
$$4 - 5x + 3 = 2y - 3 + 3$$
$$7 - 5x = 2y$$
$$\frac{7 - 5x}{2} = \frac{2y}{2}$$
$$\frac{7 - 5x}{2} = y$$

When $x = -2$
$$y = \frac{7 - 5x}{2}$$
$$y = \frac{7 - 5(-2)}{2}$$
$$y = 8\frac{1}{2}$$

3.
$$4(3x - y) = 10$$
$$12x - 4y = 10$$
$$4y = 12x - 10$$
$$\frac{4y}{4} = \frac{12x}{4} - \frac{10}{4}$$
$$y = 3x - \frac{5}{2}$$

When $x = -2$
$$y = 3(-2) - \frac{5}{2}$$
$$y = -8\frac{1}{2}$$

4.
$$7 - 3x = 2y - 0.6x$$
$$2y = 7 - 3x + 0.6x$$
$$2y = 7 - 2.4x$$
$$\frac{2y}{2} = \frac{7}{2} - \frac{2.4x}{2}$$
$$y = 3.5 - 1.2x$$

When $x = -2$
$$y = 3.5 - 1.2(-2)$$
$$y = 5.9$$

5.
$$\frac{3}{5}x - \frac{1}{3}y = 4$$
$$\frac{3}{5}x - 4 = \frac{1}{3}y$$
$$3 \cdot \frac{3}{5}x - 4 = \frac{1}{3}y \cdot 3$$
$$\frac{9}{5}x - 12 = y$$

When $x = -2$
$$y = \frac{9}{5}x - 12$$
$$y = \frac{9}{5}(-2) - 12$$
$$y = -21$$

6.
$$1.2y + 3 = 0.36x$$
$$1.2y + 3 - 3 = 0.36x - 3$$
$$1.2y = 0.36x - 3$$
$$\frac{1.2y}{1.2} = \frac{0.36x}{1.2} - \frac{3}{1.2}$$
$$y = 0.3x - 2.5$$
When $x = -2$
$$y = 0.3(-2) - 2.5$$
$$y = -3.1$$

7.
$$4y + x = 5(2x - y)$$
$$4y + x = 10x - 5y$$
$$4y + x - x = 10x - 5y - x$$
$$4y = 9x - 5y$$
$$4y + 5y = 9x - 5y + 5y$$
$$9y = 9x$$
$$\frac{9y}{9} = \frac{9x}{9}$$
$$y = x$$
When $y = 4$
$$x = 4$$

8.
$$-2(x + 3y) = x + 6y$$
$$-2x - 6y = x + 6y$$
$$-2x - 6y - x = x + 6y - x$$
$$-3x - 6y = 6y$$
$$-3x - 6y + 6y = 6y + 6y$$
$$-3x = 12y$$
$$\frac{-3x}{-3} = \frac{6y}{-3} + \frac{6y}{-3}$$
$$x = -4y$$
When $y = 4$
$$x = -4(4)$$
$$x = -16$$

9.
$$2.5(x - 2y) = 10$$
$$2.5x - 5y = 10$$
$$2.5x - 5y + 5y = 10 + 5y$$
$$2.5x = 10 + 5y$$
$$\frac{2.5x}{2.5} = \frac{10}{2.5} + \frac{5y}{2.5}$$
$$x = 4 + 2y$$
When $y = 4$
$$x = 4 + 2(4)$$
$$x = 12$$

10.
$$6y + 9 = \frac{2}{3}x$$
$$\frac{3}{2} \cdot \frac{2}{3}x = \frac{3}{2} \cdot (6y + 9)$$
$$x = 9y + 13.5$$
When $y = 4$
$$x = 9(4) + 13.5$$
$$x = 49.5$$

11.
$$\frac{2(3x - 2)}{y} = 12$$
$$\frac{6x - 4}{y} = 12$$
$$y \cdot \frac{6x - 4}{y} = 12 \cdot y$$
$$6x - 4 = 12y$$
$$6x - 4 + 4 = 12y + 4$$
$$6x = 12y + 4$$
$$\frac{6x}{6} = \frac{12y}{6} + \frac{4}{6}$$
$$x = 2y + \frac{2}{3}$$
When $y = 4$
$$x = 2(4) + \frac{2}{3}$$
$$x = 8\frac{2}{3}$$

12.
$$\frac{1}{4}(3 - 2x) = \frac{3y}{8}$$
$$\frac{3}{4} - \frac{1}{2}x = \frac{3y}{8}$$
$$-\frac{3}{4} + \frac{3}{4} - \frac{1}{2}x = \frac{3y}{8}$$
$$-\frac{1}{2}x = \frac{3y}{8} - \frac{3}{4}$$
$$-2 \cdot \left(-\frac{1}{2}x\right) = \left(\frac{3y}{8} - \frac{3}{4}\right) \cdot (-2)$$
$$x = -\frac{3}{4}y + \frac{3}{2}$$
When $y = 4$
$$x = -\frac{3}{4}(4) + \frac{3}{2}$$
$$x = -\frac{3}{2}$$

13. a) $P = \frac{\pi}{2}r + 2r$

b) $r = \frac{2P}{\pi + 4}$

c) $r = \frac{2P}{\pi + 4}$
$$r = \frac{2(50)}{\frac{22}{7} + 4}$$
$$r = \frac{100}{\frac{50}{7}}$$
$$r = 100 \cdot \frac{7}{50}$$
$$r = 14$$
The radius is approximately 14 centimeters.

14. a) $N = 10 + 4x$

b) $x = \dfrac{N - 10}{4}$

c) $x = \dfrac{N - 10}{4}$

$x = \dfrac{150 - 10}{4}$

$x = 35$

15. a) $F = \dfrac{9}{5}(C) + 32$

b)

F	77	104	131
C	25	40	55

When: C = 25:

$F = \dfrac{9}{5}(C) + 32$

$F = \dfrac{9}{5}(25) + 32$

$F = 77$

When C = 40:

$F = \dfrac{9}{5}(C) + 32$

$F = \dfrac{9}{5}(40) + 32$

$F = 104$

When C = 55:

$F = \dfrac{9}{5}(C) + 32$

$F = \dfrac{9}{5}(55) + 32$

$F = 131$

c) $F = \dfrac{9}{5}(C) + 32$

$F = \dfrac{9}{5}(37) + 32$

$F = 98.6$

Normal body temperature is 98.6°F.

16. a) $t = \dfrac{H - 8}{6}$ or $t = \dfrac{H}{6} - \dfrac{4}{3}$

b)

Height (H centimeters)	14	20	26	32
Time (t months)	1	2	3	4

When $t = 1$:

$H = 2\,[4 + 3(1)]$

$H = 14$

When $H = 20$:

$t = \dfrac{H - 8}{6}$

$t = \dfrac{20 - 8}{6}$

$t = 2$

When $H = 26$:

$t = \dfrac{H - 8}{6}$

$t = \dfrac{26 - 8}{6}$

$t = 3$

When $t = 4$:

$H = 2[4 + 3(4)]$

$H = 32$

c) When $t = 6$:

$H = 2[4 + 3(6)]$

$H = 44$

d) When $H = 29$:

$t = \dfrac{H - 8}{6}$

$t = \dfrac{29 - 8}{6}$

$t = 3\dfrac{1}{2}$

It will take $3\dfrac{1}{2}$ months for the sapling to grow to a height of 59 centimeters.

17. a) $P = 4\left[\frac{1}{3}(x + 2)\right]$

b) $x = \frac{3P - 8}{4}$

c)

P	4	8	12	16
x	1	4	7	10

When $P = 4$:

$x = \frac{3P - 8}{4}$

$x = \frac{3(4) - 8}{4}$

$x = 1$

When $P = 8$:

$x = \frac{3P - 8}{4}$

$x = \frac{3(8) - 8}{4}$

$x = 4$

When $P = 12$:

$x = \frac{3P - 8}{4}$

$x = \frac{3(12) - 8}{4}$

$x = 7$

When $P = 16$:

$x = \frac{3P - 8}{4}$

$x = \frac{3(16) - 8}{4}$

$x = 10$

d) When $P = 52$:

$x = \frac{3P - 8}{4}$

$x = \frac{3(52) - 8}{4}$

$x = 37$

The value of x is 37.

18. a) $n = \frac{360}{180 - A}$

b)

n	3	6	9	12
A	60	120	140	150

When $A = 60$:

$n = \frac{360}{180 - A}$

$n = \frac{360}{180 - 60}$

$n = 3$

When $A = 120$:

$n = \frac{360}{180 - A}$

$n = \frac{360}{180 - 120}$

$n = 6$

When $A = 140$:

$n = \frac{360}{180 - A}$

$n = \frac{360}{180 - 140}$

$n = 9$

When $A = 150$:

$n = \frac{360}{180 - A}$

$n = \frac{360}{180 - 150}$

$n = 12$

c) $n = \frac{360}{180 - A}$

When $A = 156$:

$n = \frac{360}{180 - 156}$

$n = 15$

The regular polygon has 15 sides.

Brain@Work

1. $\frac{p + 3}{p - 3} = \frac{3}{2} + 1$

$\frac{p + 3}{p - 3} = \frac{5}{2}$

$5(p - 3) = 2(p + 3)$

$5p - 15 = 2p + 6$

$3p = 21$

$p = 7$

2. Let x be the number of students in Mrs. Duffy's class.

$7x + 26 = 10x - 25$

$3x = 51$

$x = 17$

There are 17 students in Mrs. Duffy's class

Number of almonds she roasted $= 7(17) + 26$

$= 119 + 26$

$= 145$

She roasted 145 almonds.

Chapter 4

Lesson 4.1

1. Slope $= \dfrac{4 - (-1)}{-1 - 3} = -\dfrac{5}{4}$

2. Slope $= \dfrac{-2 - (-2)}{3 - (-2)} = 0$

3. Slope $= \dfrac{4 - 0}{2 - (-1)} = \dfrac{4}{3}$

4. Slope $= \dfrac{3 - (-2)}{-1 - (-1)} = \dfrac{5}{0}$ undefined

5. Slope $= \dfrac{(-3) - 5}{0 - 4} = \dfrac{-8}{-4} = 2$

6. Slope $= \dfrac{8 - (-2)}{9 - 9} = \dfrac{10}{10} =$ undefined

7. Slope $= \dfrac{(-3) - 2}{(-3) - (-8)} = \dfrac{-5}{5} = -1$

8. Slope $= \dfrac{4 - 4}{3 - 7} = \dfrac{0}{-4} = 0$

9. a)

Length of P (feet)	Length of Q (feet)	Slope of Ramp
3	60	$\dfrac{P}{Q} = \dfrac{3}{60} = \dfrac{1}{20}$
5	50	$\dfrac{P}{Q} = \dfrac{5}{50} = \dfrac{1}{10}$
3	36	$\dfrac{P}{Q} = \dfrac{3}{36} = \dfrac{1}{12}$
2	30	$\dfrac{P}{Q} = \dfrac{2}{30} = \dfrac{1}{15}$

   b) $\dfrac{1}{10}, \dfrac{1}{12}, \dfrac{1}{15}, \dfrac{1}{20}$

   c) The ramp with $P = 3$ ft and $Q = 36$ ft.

Lesson 4.2

1. y-intercept $= 1$;
   Slope $= \dfrac{2 - 0}{2 - (-2)}$
   $= \dfrac{2}{4}$
   $= \dfrac{1}{2}$

2. y-intercept $= 0$;
   Slope $= \dfrac{3 - (-3)}{-2 - (2)}$
   $= -\dfrac{6}{4}$
   $= -\dfrac{3}{2}$

3. y-intercept $= 4$;
   Slope $= \dfrac{4 - (-4)}{0 - 4}$
   $= \dfrac{8}{-4}$
   $= -2$

4. y-intercept $= -1$;
   Slope $= \dfrac{2 - (-4)}{4 - (-4)}$
   $= \dfrac{6}{8}$
   $= \dfrac{3}{4}$

5. The line passes through the points $(-2, 3)$ and $(1, -3)$.

   Slope $m = \dfrac{(-3) - 3}{1 - (-2)} = \dfrac{-6}{3} = -2$

   The line intersects the y-axis at the point $(0, -1)$. So, the y-intercept, b is -1.

   Slope-intercept form: $y = (-2)x - 1$
   $\qquad\qquad\qquad\qquad\quad y = -2x - 1$

6. The line passes through the points $(-5, -2)$ and $(5, 6)$.

   Slope $m = \dfrac{6 - (-2)}{5 - (-5)} = \dfrac{8}{10} = \dfrac{4}{5}$

   The line intersects the y-axis at the point $(0, 2)$. So, the y-intercept, b is 2.

   Slope-intercept form: $y = \dfrac{4}{5}x + 2$

7. The line passes through the points $(-4, -6)$ and $(4, 6)$.

   Slope $m = \dfrac{6 - (-6)}{4 - (-4)} = \dfrac{12}{8} = \dfrac{3}{2}$

   The line intersects the y-axis at the point $(0, 0)$. So, the y-intercept, b is 0.

   Slope-intercept form: $y = \dfrac{3}{2}x + 0$
   $\qquad\qquad\qquad\qquad\qquad\quad y = \dfrac{3}{2}x$

8. The line passes through the points $(10, -1)$ and $(-10, 3)$.

   Slope $m = \dfrac{3 - (-1)}{-10 - 10} = \dfrac{4}{-20} = -\dfrac{1}{5}$

   The line intersects the y-axis at the point $(0, 1)$. So, the y-intercept, b is 1.

   Slope-intercept form: $y = -\dfrac{1}{5}x + 1$

9. $y = -2$

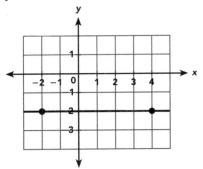

10. $x = 3$

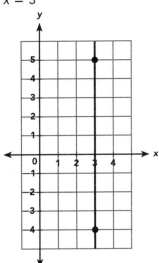

11. $x = 0$

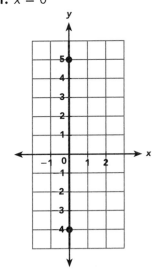

12. $y = 0$

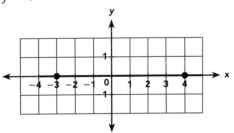

Lesson 4.3

1. Slope $= 4$; y-intercept $= -7$

2. Slope $= -1$, y-intercept $= 3$

3.
$$4x - 3y = 9$$
$$4x - 3y - 4x = 9 - 4x$$
$$-3y = 9 - 4x$$
$$\frac{-3y}{-3} = \frac{9 - 4x}{-3}$$
$$y = \frac{4}{3}x - 3$$
Slope $= \frac{4}{3}$; y-intercept $= -3$

4.
$$-5x + 2y = 6$$
$$-5x + 2y + 5x = 6 + 5x$$
$$2y = 6 + 5x$$
$$\frac{2y}{2} = \frac{6 + 5x}{2}$$
$$y = 3 + \frac{5}{2}x$$
Slope $= \frac{5}{2}$; y-intercept $= 3$

5. $y = mx + b$
$y = \frac{2}{3}x + 1$

6. $y = mx + b$
$y = -5x + 2$

7. $y = mx + b$
$-3 = 2(0) + b$
$b = -3$
So, an equation of the line is $y = 2x - 3$.

8. $y = mx + b$
$3 = 8\left(-\frac{3}{4}\right) + b$
$b = 9$
So, an equation of the line is $y = -\frac{3}{4}x + 9$.

9.
$$4x - 3y + 9 = 0$$
$$4x - 3y + 9 - 4x = 0 - 4x$$
$$-3y + 9 - 9 = -4x - 9$$
$$-3y = -4x - 9$$
$$\frac{-3y}{-3} = \frac{-4x - 9}{-3}$$
$$y = \frac{4}{3}x + 3$$
$$m = \frac{4}{3}$$
An equation of the line is $y = \frac{4}{3}x - 1$.

10.
$$5y + x = 10$$
$$5y + x - x = 10 - x$$
$$5y = 10 - x$$
$$\frac{5y}{5} = \frac{10 - x}{5}$$
$$y = 2 - \frac{1}{5}x$$
$$m = -\frac{1}{5}$$
An equation of the line is $y = -\frac{1}{5}x + 7$.

11. $2y = -3x + 1$
$$\frac{2y}{2} = \frac{-3x + 1}{2}$$
$$y = -\frac{3}{2}x + \frac{1}{2}$$
$$m = -\frac{3}{2}$$

An equation of the line is $y = -\frac{3}{2}x - 2$.

12.
$$4x = 1 + 2y$$
$$2y + 1 - 1 = 4x - 1$$
$$2y = 4x - 1$$
$$\frac{2y}{2} = \frac{4x - 1}{2}$$
$$y = 2x - \frac{1}{2}$$
$$m = 2$$
$$y = mx + b$$
$$-5 = 2(3) + b$$
$$b = -11$$
An equation of the line is $y = 2x - 11$.

13. $7y = 6x - 14$
$$\frac{7y}{7} = \frac{6x - 14}{7}$$
$$y = \frac{6}{7}x - 2$$
$$m = \frac{6}{7}$$
$$y = mx + b$$
$$0 = 7\left(\frac{6}{7}\right) + b$$
$$b = -6$$
An equation of the line is $y = \frac{6}{7}x - 6$.

14.
$$2x = 3 - 5y$$
$$3 - 5y - 3 = 2x - 3$$
$$-5y = 2x - 3$$
$$\frac{-5y}{-5} = \frac{2x - 3}{-5}$$
$$y = -\frac{2}{5}x + \frac{3}{5}$$
$$m = -\frac{2}{5}$$
$$y = mx + b$$
$$-2 = (-3)\left(-\frac{2}{5}\right) + b$$
$$b = -\frac{16}{5}$$
An equation of the line is $y = -\frac{2}{5}x - \frac{16}{5}$

15. $m = \dfrac{9 - (-6)}{-4 - 1}$
$$= \frac{15}{-5}$$
$$= -3$$
$$y = mx + b$$
$$9 = (-4)(-3) + b$$
$$b = -3$$
An equation of the line is $y = -3x - 3$.

16. $m = \dfrac{11 - (-10)}{0 - 3}$
$$= \frac{21}{-3}$$
$$= -7$$
$$y = mx + b$$
$$11 = (0)(-7) + b$$
$$b = 11$$
An equation of the line is $y = -7x + 11$.

17. $m = \dfrac{-7 - (-9)}{2 - (-5)}$

$\quad = \dfrac{2}{7}$

$y = mx + b$

$-7 = (2)\left(\dfrac{2}{7}\right) + b$

$b = -\dfrac{53}{7}$

An equation of the line is $y = \dfrac{2}{7}x - \dfrac{53}{7}$.

Lesson 4.4

1.

x	−3	0	3
y	0	2	4

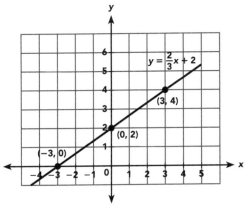

2.

x	−4	0	4
y	−8	−5	−2

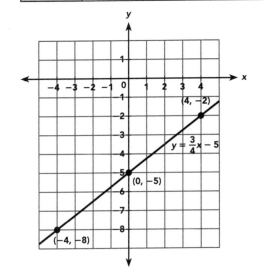

3.

x	−5	0	5
y	0	3	6

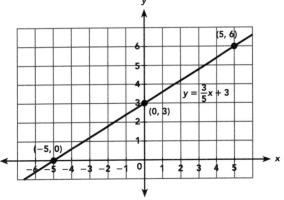

4.

x	−2	0	2
y	9	5	1

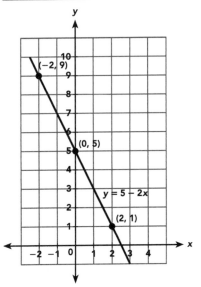

5.

x	−6	0	6
y	3	2	1

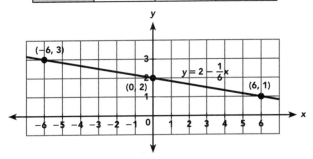

6.

x	−3	0	3
y	−8	−4	0

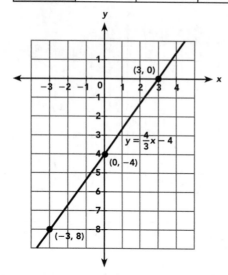

7.

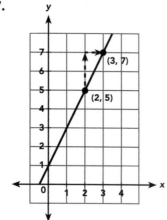

8.

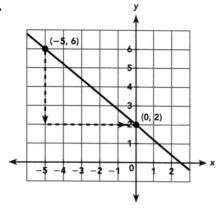

9.

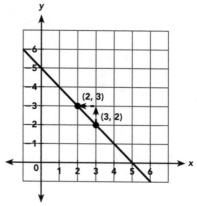

10.

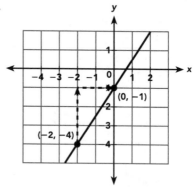

Lesson 4.5

1. a) From the graph, the vertical intercept is 5. It represents the initial fixed amount for renting a bike.

   b) The graph passes through (0, 5) and (6, 20).

   $$\text{Slope} = \frac{20 - 5}{6 - 0} = \frac{15}{6} = \frac{5}{2}$$

   The line has slope $m = \frac{5}{2}$. It represents the hourly rate for renting a bike.

   It costs Max $20 to rent a bike for 6 hours.

2. a) From the graph, the initial height of sapling A is 40 centimeters and that of sapling B is 20 centimeters.

   b) Sapling B. The graph of sapling B passes through (0, 20) and (4, 40).

   $$\text{Slope} = \frac{40 - 20}{4 - 0} = \frac{20}{4} = 5$$

   So, the growth for sapling B is 5 centimeters.

   The graph of sapling A passes through (0, 40) and (3, 50).

   $$\text{Slope} = \frac{50 - 40}{3 - 0} = \frac{10}{3} = 3\frac{1}{3}$$

   So, the growth of sapling A is $3\frac{1}{3}$ centimeters.

3. a) From the graph, the vertical intercept is 100. It represents the initial rental charges of the concert hall.

b) The graph passes through (0, 100) and (6, 400).

$$\text{Slope} = \frac{400 - 100}{6 - 0} = \frac{300}{6} = 50$$

The slope represents the hourly rental charges of the concert hall. It is $50.

4. a) From the graph, the initial amount of water in container P is 1,000 milliliters and that in container Q is 800 milliliters.

b) The graph of P passes through (0, 1,000) and (40, 400).

$$\text{Slope of P} = \frac{1,000 - 400}{0 - 40} = \frac{600}{-40} = -15$$

The graph of Q passes through (0, 800) and (40, 400).

$$\text{Slope of Q} = \frac{800 - 400}{0 - 40} = \frac{400}{-40} = -10$$

15 milliliters of water is leaking from container P per minute while 10 milliliters of water is leaking from container Q per minute. So, container P has a bigger hole.

5. a)

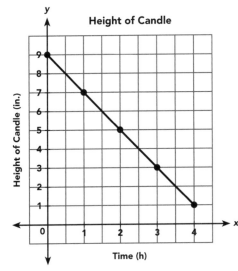

b) From the graph, the vertical intercept is 9. It represents the initial height of the candle.

c) $\text{Slope} = \dfrac{9 - 7}{0 - 1} = -2$

The slope represents the rate at which the candle burns.

d) $y = mx + b$

$9 = 0(-2) + b$

$b = 9$

An equation of the line is $y = -2x + 9$.

Brain@Work

1. a) Let the speed of the bus as it passes the stop be a meters per second.

The area under the speed-time graph is the distance traveled by the bus. So, the area is 50 square units.

Area of trapezium = 50

$$\frac{1}{2}(5 - 0)(a + 8) = 50$$

$$\frac{5(a + 8)}{2} = 50$$

$$\frac{5(a + 8)}{2} \cdot 2 = 50 \cdot 2$$

$$5(a + 8) = 100$$

$$\frac{5(a + 8)}{5} = \frac{100}{5}$$

$$a + 8 = 20$$

$$a + 8 - 8 = 20 - 8$$

$$a = 12$$

So, the speed of the bus as it passes the stop is 12 meters per second.

b) Rate of slowing down = slope of the graph

$$= \frac{12 - 8}{0 - 5}$$

$$= -\frac{4}{5}$$

$$= -0.8$$

The rate of deceleration is 0.8 meter per square second.

c) An equation of the line is $y = -0.8t + 12$.

2. a) The speed of the car is increasing.

b) The car is slowing down.

c) The car is not moving.

d) The speed of the car is increasing.

e) The car is slowing down.

f) The car is not moving.

Cumulative Practice for Chapters 3 to 4

1. $3(2x - 4) - 7 = 23$

$6x - 12 - 7 = 23$

$6x - 19 = 23$

$6x - 19 + 19 = 23 + 19$

$6x = 42$

$$\frac{6x}{6} = \frac{42}{6}$$

$x = 7$

2. $5x - (8 - 3x) = 72$

$5x - 8 + 3x = 72$

$8x - 3 = 72$

$8x - 8 + 8 = 72 + 8$

$8x = 80$

$x = 10$

3. $\dfrac{1}{6}(x + 3) - 4 = -3.2$

$\dfrac{1}{6}(x + 3) - 4 + 4 = -3.2 + 4$

$\dfrac{(x + 3)}{6} = 0.8$

$\dfrac{x}{6} + \dfrac{3}{6} = 0.8$

$\dfrac{x}{6} + 0.5 = 0.8$

$\dfrac{x}{6} + 0.5 - 0.5 = 0.8 - 0.5$

$\dfrac{x}{6} = 0.3$

$\dfrac{x}{6} \cdot 6 = 0.3 \cdot 6$

$x = 1.8$

4. $2x - \dfrac{5}{9} = \dfrac{7x + 8}{9}$

$\dfrac{18x - 5}{9} = \dfrac{7x + 8}{9}$

$\dfrac{18x - 5}{9} \cdot 9 = \dfrac{7x + 8}{9} \cdot 9$

$18x - 5 = 7x + 8$

$18x - 5 + 5 = 7x + 8 + 5$

$18x = 7x + 13$

$18x - 7x = 7x - 7x + 13$

$11x = 13$

$\dfrac{11x}{11} = \dfrac{13}{11}$

$x = \dfrac{13}{11}$

5. Let $x = 0.\overline{8}$.

$x = 0.888\ 888\ldots$

$10x = 8.888\ 888\ldots$

$10x - x = 8.\overline{8} - 0.\overline{8}$

$9x = 8$

$\dfrac{9x}{9} = \dfrac{8}{9}$

$x = \dfrac{8}{9}$

6. Let $x = 0.\overline{54}$.

$x = 0.54\ 54\ 54\ldots$

$100x = 54.54\ 54\ 54\ldots$

$100x - x = 54.\overline{54} - 0.\overline{54}$

$99x = 54$

$\dfrac{99x}{99} = \dfrac{54}{99}$

$x = \dfrac{54}{99}$

$= \dfrac{6}{11}$

7. Let $x = 0.4\overline{6}$.

$x = 0.46\ 66\ 66\ldots$

$10x = 4.66\ 66\ 66\ldots$

$10x - x = 4.\overline{6} - 0.4\overline{6}$

$9x = 4.2$

$\dfrac{9x}{9} = \dfrac{4.2}{9}$

$x = \dfrac{42}{90}$

$= \dfrac{7}{15}$

8. Let $x = 0.74\overline{1}$.

$x = 0.74\ 11\ 11\ldots$

$100x = 74.11\ 11\ 11\ldots$

$100x - x = 74.\overline{1} - 0.74\overline{1}$

$99x = 74.11 - 0.74$

$99x = 73.37$

$x = \dfrac{73.37}{99}$

$= \dfrac{7,337}{9,900}$

$= \dfrac{667}{900}$

9. $8 - 5x \overset{?}{=} 11x - 24$

$8 - 8 - 5x \overset{?}{=} 11x - 24 - 8$

$-5x \overset{?}{=} 11x - 32$

$-5x - 11x \overset{?}{=} 11x - 11x - 32$

$-16x \overset{?}{=} -32$

$\dfrac{-16x}{16} \overset{?}{=} \dfrac{-32}{-16}$

$x = 2$

The equation has one solution.

10.
$$8x + 6 \stackrel{?}{=} 3\left(\frac{8}{3}x + 2\right)$$
$$\frac{8x + 6}{3} \stackrel{?}{=} \frac{8}{3}x + 2$$
$$\frac{8}{3}x + 2 \stackrel{?}{=} \frac{8}{3}x + 2$$
$$\frac{8}{3}x - \frac{8}{3}x + 2 \stackrel{?}{=} \frac{8}{3}x - \frac{8}{3}x + 2$$
$$2 = 2$$

Because $2 = 2$ is always true, the equation has infinitely many solutions.

11.
$$14 - (12 - 4y) \stackrel{?}{=} \frac{1}{2}(8y + 3)$$
$$14 - 12 + 4y \stackrel{?}{=} \frac{1}{2}(8y + 3)$$
$$2 + 4y \stackrel{?}{=} \frac{1}{2}(8y + 3)$$
$$2(2 + 4y) \stackrel{?}{=} 8y + 3$$
$$4 + 8y \stackrel{?}{=} 8y + 3$$
$$4 \neq 3$$

Because $4 \neq 3$, the equation has no solution.

12.
$$9y + 8 \stackrel{?}{=} 4\left(y - \frac{3}{4}\right)$$
$$9y + 8 \stackrel{?}{=} 4y - 3$$
$$9y - 4y + 8 \stackrel{?}{=} 4y - 4y - 3$$
$$5y + 8 \stackrel{?}{=} -3$$
$$5y + 8 - 8 \stackrel{?}{=} -3 - 8$$
$$5y \stackrel{?}{=} -11$$
$$\frac{5y}{5} \stackrel{?}{=} -\frac{11}{5}$$
$$y = -\frac{11}{5}$$

The equation has one solution.

13.
$$5x + 13 = 4 + y$$
$$5(-3) + 13 = 4 + y$$
$$-15 + 13 = 4 + y$$
$$-2 = 4 + y$$
$$-2 - 4 = 4 - 4 + y$$
$$y = -6$$

14.
$$7x - 3y = 6$$
$$7(-3) - 3y = 6$$
$$-21 - 3y = 6$$
$$-21 + 21 - 3y = 6 + 21$$
$$-3y = 27$$
$$\frac{-3y}{3} = \frac{27}{-3}$$
$$y = -9$$

15.
$$2x - 3y = \frac{1}{4}(x - 13)$$
$$2(-3) - 3y = \frac{1}{4}(-3 - 13)$$
$$-6 - 3y = -4$$
$$-6 + 6 - 3y = -4 + 6$$
$$-3y = 2$$
$$\frac{-3y}{3} = \frac{2}{-3}$$
$$y = -\frac{2}{3}$$
$$\frac{2}{9}(3y + 4x) = 2x$$

16.
$$\frac{2}{9}[3y + 4(-3)] = 2(-3)$$
$$\frac{2}{9}(3y - 12) = -6$$
$$9 \cdot \frac{2}{9}(3y - 12) = (-6) \cdot 9$$
$$2(3y - 12) = -54$$
$$\frac{2(3y - 12)}{2} = -54$$
$$3y - 12 = -27$$
$$3y - 12 + 12 = -27 + 12$$
$$3y = -15$$
$$\frac{3y}{3} = -\frac{15}{3}$$
$$y = -5$$

17.
$$\frac{5x - 3}{2y} = -\frac{3}{5}$$
$$\frac{5(-3) - 3}{2y} = -\frac{3}{5}$$
$$\frac{-15 - 3}{2y} = -\frac{3}{5}$$
$$\frac{-18}{2y} = -\frac{3}{5}$$
$$\frac{-9}{y} = -\frac{3}{5}$$
$$\frac{9}{y} = \frac{3}{5}$$
$$\frac{9}{y} \cdot y = \frac{3}{5} \cdot y$$
$$9 = \frac{3y}{5}$$
$$9 \cdot 5 = \frac{3y}{5} \cdot 5$$
$$45 = 3y$$
$$\frac{45}{3} = \frac{3y}{3}$$
$$15 = y$$
$$y = 15$$

18.
$$\frac{7y - 4}{2} = 3x$$
$$\frac{7y - 4}{2} = 3(-3)$$
$$\frac{7y - 4}{2} = -9$$
$$\frac{7y - 4}{2} \cdot 2 = (-9) \cdot 2$$
$$7y - 4 = -18$$
$$7y - 4 + 4 = -18 + 4$$
$$7y = -14$$
$$\frac{7y}{7} = -\frac{14}{7}$$
$$y = -2$$

19.
$$6x + 7y = 2(5x + y)$$
$$6x + 7y = 10x + 2y$$
$$6x - 6x + 7y = 10x - 6x + 2y$$
$$7y = 4x + 2y$$
$$7y - 2y = 4x + 2y - 2y$$
$$5y = 4x$$
$$\frac{5y}{4} = \frac{4x}{4}$$
$$\frac{5y}{4} = x$$
$$x = \frac{5y}{4}$$
$$= \frac{5(4)}{4}$$
$$= 5$$

20.
$$x + 9y = 6(x - y)$$
$$x + 9y = 6x - 6y$$
$$x - x + 9y = 6x - x - 6y$$
$$9y = 5x - 6y$$
$$9y + 6y = 5x - 6y + 6y$$
$$15y = 5x$$
$$\frac{15y}{5} = \frac{5x}{5}$$
$$3y = x$$
$$x = 3(4)$$
$$= 12$$

21.
$$\frac{3}{4}y - \frac{7}{8}x = 10$$
$$\frac{3}{4}y - \frac{7}{8}x - \frac{3}{4}y = 10 - \frac{3}{4}y$$
$$-\frac{7}{8}x = 10 - \frac{3}{4}y$$
$$-\frac{7}{8}x = \frac{40}{4} - \frac{3}{4}y$$
$$-7x = \frac{40 - 3y}{4} \cdot 8$$
$$-7x = 2(40 - 3y)$$
$$-7x = 80 - 6y$$

$$\frac{-7x}{-7} = \frac{80 - 6y}{-7}$$
$$x = \frac{-(6y - 80)}{-7}$$
$$= \frac{6y - 80}{7}$$
When $y = 4$,
$$x = \frac{6(4) - 80}{7}$$
$$= -8$$

22.
$$\frac{0.7(4x + 3)}{y} = 14$$
$$\frac{0.7(4x + 3)}{y} \cdot y = 14 \cdot y$$
$$0.7(4x + 3) = 14y$$
$$\frac{0.7(4x + 3)}{0.7} = \frac{14y}{0.7}$$
$$4x + 3 = 20y$$
$$x + 3 - 3 = 20y - 3$$
$$4x = 20y - 3$$
$$x = \frac{20y - 3}{4}$$
$$x = 5(4) - 0.75$$
$$= 19.25$$

23.
$$0.5(2x + y) = 12 - 3x$$
$$\frac{1}{2}(2x + y) = 12 - 3x$$
$$2x + y = 24 - 6x$$
$$2x + 6x + y = 24 - 6x + 6x$$
$$8x + y = 24$$
$$8x + y - y = 24 - y$$
$$8x = 24 - y$$
$$\frac{8x}{8} = \frac{24 - y}{8}$$
$$x = 3 - \frac{y}{8}$$
When $y = 4$,
$$x = 3 - \frac{4}{8}$$
$$= 2\frac{1}{2}$$

24.
$$\frac{3y + x}{4} + \frac{y}{2} = 10$$
$$\frac{3y + x}{4} + \frac{2y}{4} = 10$$
$$\frac{3y + x + 2y}{4} = 10$$
$$5y + x = 40$$
$$x = 40 - 5y$$
When $y = 4$, $x = 50 - 5(4) = 30$

25. The graph passes through the points $(0, 6)$ and $(8, 0)$.

$$\text{Slope} = \frac{\text{Rise}}{\text{Run}}$$
$$= \frac{0 - 6}{8 - 0}$$
$$= -\frac{6}{8}$$
$$= -\frac{3}{4}$$

The line intersects the y-axis at the point $(0, 6)$. So, the y-intercept is 6.

So, the equation of the line is $y = -\frac{3}{4}x + 6$.

26. The graph passes through the points $(0, 3)$ and $(6, 15)$.

$$\text{Slope} = \frac{\text{Rise}}{\text{Run}}$$
$$= \frac{15 - 3}{6 - 0}$$
$$= \frac{12}{6}$$
$$= 2$$

The line intersects the y-axis at the point $(0, 3)$. So, the y-intercept is 3.
So, the equation of the line is $y = 2x + 3$.

27. The graph passes through the points $(-4, 8)$ and $(0, 0)$.

$$\text{Slope} = \frac{\text{Rise}}{\text{Run}}$$
$$= \frac{0 - 8}{0 - (-4)}$$
$$= \frac{-8}{4}$$
$$= -2$$

The line intersects the y-axis at the point $(0, 0)$. So, the y-intercept is 0.
So, the equation of the line is $y = -2x$.

28. The graph passes through the points $(-1, -4)$ and $(5, -4)$.

$$\text{Slope} = \frac{\text{Rise}}{\text{Run}}$$
$$= \frac{-4 - (-4)}{5 - (-1)}$$
$$= \frac{0}{6}$$
$$= 0$$

The line intersects the y-axis at the point $(0, -4)$. So, the y-intercept is -4.
So, the equation of the line is $y = -4$.

29. Slope, $m = -\frac{4}{3}$

y-intercept, $b = 0$.

30. Slope, $m = 9$.
y-intercept, $b = -4$.

31. $y = -\frac{2}{3}$.

32. $y = -\frac{1}{4}x + 5$.

33.
$$3x + 5 = 2y$$
$$3x + 5 - 5 = 2y - 5$$
$$3x = 2y$$
$$\frac{3x}{2} = \frac{2y}{2}$$
$$\frac{3x}{2} = y$$
$$y = \frac{3}{2}x$$

The line has slope $m = \frac{3}{2}$.

So, the line parallel to $3x + 5 = 2y$ has slope $\frac{3}{2}$.

Substituting $m = \frac{3}{2}$ and $b = -1$ in the slope-intercept form $y = mx + c$ gives:

$$y = \frac{3}{2} \cdot x + (-1)$$
$$= \frac{3}{2}x - 1$$

So, an equation of the line parallel to $3x + 5 = 2y$ is $y = \frac{3}{2}x - 1$.

34.
$$y = mx + b$$
$$9 = 7(1) + b$$
$$9 = 7 + b$$
$$9 - 7 = 7 - 7 + b$$
$$2 = b$$

The y-intercept is 2.
$$y = mx + b$$
$$y = 7x + 2$$
So, an equation of the line is $y = 7x + 2$.

35.
$$3y - 2x = 6$$
$$3y - 2x + 2x = 6 + 2x$$
$$3y = 6 + 2x$$
$$\frac{3y}{3} = \frac{6 + 2x}{3}$$
$$y = 2 + \frac{2}{3}x$$

The line has slope $m = \frac{2}{3}$.
So, the line parallel to $3y - 2x = 6$ has slope $\frac{2}{3}$.
Then, write the equation of a line that passes through $(0, 0)$ and has slope $m = \frac{2}{3}$.

$$y = mx + b$$
$$0 = \frac{2}{3}(0) + b$$
$$b = 0$$

The y-intercept is 0.
So, the equation of the line is $y = \frac{2}{3}x$.

36.
$$y + 8x = 0$$
$$y + 8x - 8x = -8x$$
$$y = -8x$$
The line has slope $m = -8$.
So, the line parallel to $y + 8x = 0$ has slope $m = -8$.
$$y = mx + b$$
$$2 = -8(0) + b$$
$$b = 2$$
The y-intercept is 2.
So, the equation of the line is $y = -8x + 2$.

37. Let $(1, 6)$ be (x_1, y_1) and $(5, 9)$ be (x_2, y_2).
$$\text{Slope} = \frac{y_2 - y_1}{x_2 - x_1}$$
$$= \frac{9 - 6}{5 - 1}$$
$$= \frac{3}{4}$$
The line has slope $m = \frac{3}{4}$.
$$y = mx + b$$
$$6 = \frac{3}{4}(1) + b$$
$$6 - \frac{3}{4} = \frac{3}{4} - \frac{3}{4} + b$$
$$\frac{24}{4} - \frac{3}{4} = b$$
$$\frac{21}{4} = b$$
The y-intercept is $\frac{21}{4}$.
So, an equation of the line is $y = \frac{3}{4}x + \frac{21}{4}$, or $4y = 3x + 21$.

38. Let $(3, 2)$ be (x_1, y_1) and $(7, -3)$ be (x_2, y_2).
$$\text{Slope} = \frac{y_2 - y_1}{x_2 - x_1}$$
$$= \frac{-3 - 2}{7 - 3}$$
$$= -\frac{5}{4}$$
The line has slope $m = -\frac{5}{4}$.
$$y = mx + b$$
$$2 = -\frac{5}{4}(3) + b$$
$$2 = -\frac{15}{4} + b$$
$$2 + \frac{15}{4} = -\frac{15}{4} + \frac{15}{4} + b$$
$$\frac{8}{4} + \frac{15}{4} = b$$
$$\frac{23}{4} = b$$
$$b = \frac{23}{4}$$

The y-intercept is $\frac{23}{4}$.

So, an equation of the line is $y = -\frac{5}{4}x + \frac{23}{4}$, or $4y = -5x + 23$.

39.

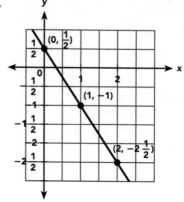

40.

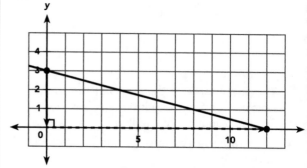

41. $2x° + 3x° + 10° = 180°$ (int. $\angle$s, // lines)
$$5x + 10 = 180$$
$$5x + 10 - 10 = 180 - 10$$
$$5x = 170$$
$$\frac{5x}{5} = \frac{170}{5}$$
$$x = 34$$

42. a) Each adult ticket costs \$7.

So, each child ticket costs $\$\frac{7}{2}$ or \$3.50.

$$C = 7 \cdot 2 + \frac{7}{2}n$$
$$C = 14 + \frac{7}{2}n$$

b)

$$C = 14 + \frac{7n}{2}$$

$$C - 14 = 14 - 14 + \frac{7n}{2}$$

$$C - 14 = \frac{7n}{2}$$

$$(C - 14) \cdot 2 = \frac{7n}{2} \cdot 2$$

$$C - 28 = 7n$$

$$\frac{C - 28}{7} = \frac{7n}{7}$$

$$n = \frac{C - 28}{7}$$

c)

$$n = \frac{2C - 28}{7}$$

$$= \frac{2(35) - 28}{7}$$

$$= \frac{70 - 28}{7}$$

$$= \frac{42}{7}$$

$$= 6$$

6 children attended the concert.

43. a) Each box of mints costs $6.
So, n boxes of mints cost $6n$.
$$\$y = \$50 - \$6n$$
$$y = 50 - 6n$$

b)
$$y + 6n = 50 - 6n + 6n$$
$$y + 6n = 50$$
$$y - y + 6n = 50 - y$$
$$6n = 50 - y$$
$$\frac{6n}{6} = \frac{50 - y}{6}$$
$$n = \frac{50 - y}{6}$$

c) When $y = 26$,
$$n = \frac{50 - 26}{6}$$
$$= \frac{24}{6}$$
$$= 4$$
Gwen bought 4 boxes of mints if she received $26 change.

d)
$$50 - 6n \overset{?}{=} 100 - 6n$$
$$50 - 6n + 6n \overset{?}{=} 100 - 6n + 6n$$
$$50 \neq 100$$
Because $50 \neq 100$, the equation has no solution. Therefore the equation is inconsistent.

44. a)
$$E = 0.4L + 50$$
$$E - 50 = 0.4L + 50 - 50$$
$$E - 50 = 0.4L$$
$$L = \frac{E - 50}{0.4}$$
$$= \frac{5}{2}(E - 50)$$

b) When $E = 90$, $L = \frac{5}{2}(90 - 50) = 100$

When $E = 130$, $L = \frac{5}{2}(130 - 50) = 200$

When $E = 170$, $L = \frac{5}{2}(170 - 50) = 300$

When $E = 210$, $L = \frac{5}{2}(210 - 50) = 400$

So the table of values is:

E Newtons	90	130	170	210
L Newtons	100	200	300	400

45. a) P: $20; Q: $40
b) The fee per minute is equivalent to the slope of each straight line graph.

Slope of $P = \frac{\text{Rise}}{\text{Run}}$

$$= \frac{60 - 20}{100 - 0}$$

$$= \frac{40}{100}$$

$$= \frac{2}{5}$$

Slope of $Q = \frac{\text{Rise}}{\text{Run}}$

$$= \frac{60 - 40}{100 - 0}$$

$$= \frac{20}{100}$$

$$= \frac{1}{5}$$

Slope of Q < slope of P. Mobile provider Q charges a lesser per minute fee.

46. a) The vertical intercept indicates the amount of water at $t = 0$, that is, the capacity of the water tank. From the given information, the capacity of the water tank is 250 gallons.

b) Slope $= \frac{\text{Rise}}{\text{Run}}$

$$= \frac{250 - 0}{0 - 50}$$

$$= -5$$

Water is leaking out of the tank at a constant rate of 5 gallons per minute.

Chapter 5

Lesson 5.1

1. $x + 3y = 6$

x	1	2	3
y	$\frac{5}{3}$	$\frac{4}{3}$	1

$2x - 3y = 3$

x	1	2	3
y	$-\frac{1}{3}$	$\frac{1}{3}$	1

Only the pair of values $x = 3$ and $y = 1$ appear in both tables. So the solution of the system of equations is $x = 3$ and $y = 1$.

2. $2x - y = 1$

x	1	2	3
y	1	3	5

$2x + 3y = 13$

x	1	2	3
y	$\frac{11}{3}$	3	$\frac{7}{3}$

Only the pair of values $x = 2$ and $y = 3$ appear in both tables. So the solution of the system of equations is $x = 2$ and $y = 3$.

3. $3x - y = 2$

x	0	1	2
y	−2	1	4

$2x = y$

x	0	1	2
y	2	0	4

Only the pair of values $x = 2$ and $y = 4$ appear in both tables. So the solution of the system of equations is $x = 2$ and $y = 4$.

4. $x + 3y = -4$

x	3	4	5
y	$-\frac{7}{3}$	$-\frac{8}{3}$	−3

$x + y = 2$

x	3	4	5
y	−1	−2	−3

Only the pair of values $x = 5$ and $y = -3$ appear in both tables. So the solution of the system of equations is $x = 5$ and $y = -3$.

5. $2x + y = 10$

x	2	3	4
y	6	4	2

$2x - y = 6$

x	2	3	4
y	−2	0	2

Only the pair of values $x = 4$ and $y = 2$ appear in both tables. So the solution of the system of equations is $x = 4$ and $y = 2$.

6. $x - y = -2$

x	0	1	2
y	2	3	4

$3x + y = 6$

x	0	1	2
y	6	3	0

Only the pair of values $x = 1$ and $y = 3$ appear in both tables. So the solution of the system of equations is $x = 1$ and $y = 3$.

7. $2y - x = 8$

x	0	1	2
y	4	4.5	5

$2x - y = -1$

x	0	1	2
y	1	3	5

Only the pair of values $x = 2$ and $y = 5$ appear in both tables. So the solution of the system of equations is $x = 2$ and $y = 5$.

8. $3x + 4y = 15$

x	0	1	2
y	3.75	3	2.25

$3x = y$

x	0	1	2
y	0	3	6

Only the pair of values $x = 1$ and $y = 3$ appear in both tables. So the solution of the system of equations is $x = 1$ and $y = 3$.

9. $5x + 4y = 64$

x	6	7	8
y	8.5	7.25	6

$3x + 8y = 72$

x	6	7	8
y	$\frac{27}{4}$	$\frac{51}{8}$	6

Only the pair of values $x = 8$ and $y = 6$ appear in both tables. So the solution of the system of equations is $x = 8$ and $y = 6$. Jolene took 8 minutes to fold a paper airplane and 6 minutes to fold a paper star.

10. $2x = 9y$

x	0	8	9
y	0	$\frac{16}{9}$	2

$2x + 3y = 24$

x	0	8	9
y	8	$\frac{8}{3}$	2

Only the pair of values $x = 9$ and $y = 2$ appear in both tables. So the solution of the system of equations is $x = 9$ and $y = 2$.
$2x = 2 \cdot 9 = 18$
$3y = 3 \cdot 2 = 6$
At the present time, Janice is 18 years old and Jennifer is 6 years old.

11. $2x + y = 18$

x	1	2	3
y	16	14	12

$2x + 3y = 42$

x	1	2	3
y	$\frac{40}{3}$	$\frac{38}{3}$	12

Only the pair of values $x = 3$ and $y = 12$ appear in both tables. So the solution of the system of equations is $x = 3$ and $y = 12$.
Difference $= 12 - 3 = 9$
The difference between Jack's walking speed and cycling speed is 9 mi/h.

Lesson 5.2

1. $3y - x = 2$ — Equation 1
$3y + x = 16$ — Equation 2
Add Equation 1 and Equation 2:
$(3y - x) + (3y + x) = 2 + 16$
$3y + 3y - x + x = 18$
$6y = 18$
$y = 3$
Substitute $y = 3$ into Equation 1:
$3(3) - x = 2$
$9 - x = 2$
$x = 7$
So the solution of the system of linear equations is $x = 7$ and $y = 3$.

2. $x - 5y = 13$ — Equation 1
$9y - x = -17$ — Equation 2
Add Equation 1 and Equation 2:
$(x - 5y) + (9y - x) = 13 + (-17)$
$x - x - 5y + 9y = 13 - 17$
$4y = -4$
$y = -1$
Substitute $y = -1$ into Equation 1:
$x - 5(-1) = 13$
$x + 5 = 13$
$x = 8$
So the solution of the system of linear equations is $x = 8$ and $y = -1$.

3. $7q + 2p = 29$ — Equation 1
$2p - q = 5$ — Equation 2
Subtract Equation 2 from Equation 1:
$(7q + 2p) - (2p - q) = 29 - 5$
$7q + q + 2p - 2p = 24$
$8q = 24$
$q = 3$
Substitute $q = 3$ into Equation 1:
$7(3) + 2p = 29$
$21 + 2p = 29$
$2p = 8$
$p = 4$
So the solution of the system of linear equations is $p = 4$ and $q = 3$.

4. $2w - 3v = 4$ — Equation 1

$w + 3v = 29$ — Equation 2

Add Equation 1 and Equation 2:

$(2w - 3v) + (w + 3v) = 4 + 29$

$2w + w - 3v + 3v = 33$

$3w = 33$

$w = 11$

Substitute $w = 11$ into Equation 1:

$2(11) - 3v = 4$

$22 - 3v = 4$

$3v = 18$

$v = 6$

So the solution of the system of linear equations is $v = 6$ and $w = 11$.

5. $2a - b = 6$ — Equation 1

$3a + b = 19$ — Equation 2

Add Equation 1 and Equation 2:

$(2a - b) + (3a + b) = 6 + 19$

$2a + 3a - b + b = 25$

$5a = 25$

$a = 5$

Substitute $a = 5$ into Equation 1:

$2(5) - b = 6$

$10 - b = 6$

$b = 4$

So the solution of the system of linear equations is $a = 5$ and $b = 4$.

6. $6n - m = 3$ — Equation 1

$3m - 6n = 15$ — Equation 2

Add Equation 1 and Equation 2:

$(6n - m) + (3m - 6n) = 3 + 15$

$6n - 6n - m + 3m = 18$

$2m = 18$

$m = 9$

Substitute $m = 9$ into Equation 1:

$6n - 9 = 3$

$6n = 12$

$n = 2$

So the solution of the system of linear equations is $m = 9$ and $n = 2$.

7. $8x + 6y = 14$ — Equation 1

$6x + 3y = 6$ — Equation 2

Multiply Equation 2 by 2:

$2(6x + 3y) = 2(6)$

$12x + 6y = 12$ — Equation 3

Subtract Equation 3 from Equation 1:

$(8x + 6y) - (12x + 6y) = 14 - 12$

$8x - 12x + 6y - 6y = 2$

$-4x = 2$

$x = -\dfrac{1}{2}$

Substitute $x = -\dfrac{1}{2}$ into Equation 1:

$8\left(-\dfrac{1}{2}\right) + 6y = 14$

$-4 + 6y = 14$

$6y = 18$

$y = 3$

So the solution of the system of linear equations is $x = -\dfrac{1}{2}$ and $y = 3$.

8. $4p + 5q = -18$ — Equation 1

$3p - 10q = 69$ — Equation 2

Multiply Equation 1 by 2:

$2(4p + 5q) = 2(-18)$

$8p + 10q = -36$ — Equation 3

Add Equation 2 and Equation 3:

$(3p - 10q) + (8p + 10q) = 69 + (-36)$

$3p + 8p - 10q + 10q = 69 - 36$

$11p = 33$

$p = 3$

Substitute $p = 3$ into Equation 1:

$4(3) + 5q = -18$

$12 + 5q = -18$

$5q = -30$

$q = -6$

So the solution of the system of linear equations is $p = 3$ and $q = -6$.

9. $3a - b = 13$ — Equation 1

$b = 2a - 7$ — Equation 2

Substitute Equation 2 into Equation 1:

$3a - (2a - 7) = 13$

$3a - 2a + 7 = 13$

$a + 7 = 13$

$a = 6$

Substitute $a = 6$ into Equation 2:

$b = 2(6) - 7$

$b = 12 - 7$

$b = 5$

So the solution of the system of linear equations is $a = 6$ and $b = 5$.

10. $5p + 3q = -7$ — Equation 1

$q = -2p + 5$ — Equation 2

Substitute Equation 2 into Equation 1:

$5p + 3(-2p + 5) = -7$

$5p - 6p + 15 = -7$

$-p = -22$

$p = 22$

Substitute $p = 22$ into Equation 2:

$q = -2(22) + 5$

$q = -44 + 5$

$q = -39$

So the solution of the system of linear equations is $p = 22$ and $q = -39$.

11. $6c - b = 5$ — Equation 1
$b - c = 5$ — Equation 2
Use Equation 2 to solve for b in terms of c:
$b - c = 5$
$\quad b = 5 + c$ — Equation 3
Substitute Equation 3 into Equation 1:
$6c - (5 + c) = 5$
$\quad 6c - 5 - c = 5$
$\qquad\qquad 5c = 10$
$\qquad\qquad\ c = 2$
Substitute $c = 2$ into Equation 3:
$b = 5 + 2$
$\ \ = 7$
So the solution of the system of linear
equations is $b = 7$ and $c = 2$.

12. $2y - x = 3$ — Equation 1
$y - x\ = 4$ — Equation 2
Use Equation 2 to solve for y in terms of x:
$y - x = 4$
$\quad y = 4 + x$ — Equation 3
Substitute Equation 3 into Equation 1:
$2(4 + x) - x = 3$
$\ 8 + 2x - x = 3$
$\qquad 8 + x = 3$
$\qquad\qquad x = -5$
Substitute $x = -5$ into Equation 3:
$y = 4 + (-5)$
$\ \ = 4 - 5$
$\ \ = -1$
So the solution of the system of linear
equations is $x = -5$ and $y = -1$.

13. $4h + k = 7$ — Equation 1
$h + 2k = 7$ — Equation 2
Use Equation 2 to solve for h in terms of k:
$h + 2k = 7$
$\qquad h = 7 - 2k$ — Equation 3
Substitute Equation 3 into Equation 1:
$4(7 - 2k) + k = 7$
$\ 28 - 8k + k = 7$
$\quad\ 28 - 7k = 7$
$\qquad\qquad 7k = 21$
$\qquad\qquad\ k = 3$
Substitute $k = 3$ into Equation 3:
$h = 7 - 2(3)$
$\ \ = 1$
So the solution of the system of linear
equations is $h = 1$ and $k = 3$.

14. $3x + 2y = 36$ — Equation 1
$5y - x = 39$ — Equation 2
Use Equation 2 to solve for x in terms of y:
$5y - x = 39$
$\qquad x = 5y - 39$ — Equation 3
Substitute Equation 3 into Equation 1:
$3(5y - 39) + 2y = 36$
$15y - 117 + 2y = 36$

$17y - 117 = 36$
$\quad\ 17y = 153$
$\qquad\ y = 9$
Substitute $y = 9$ into Equation 3:
$x = 5(9) - 39$
$\ \ = 6$
So the solution of the system of linear
equations is $x = 6$ and $y = 9$.

15. $5t + 2s = -3$ — Equation 1
$7t - 2s = 15$ — Equation 2
Use Equation 2 to solve for $2s$ in terms of t:
$7t - 2s = 15$
$\qquad 2s = 7t - 15$ — Equation 3
Substitute Equation 3 into Equation 1:
$5t + 7t - 15 = -3$
$\quad\ 12t - 15 = -3$
$\qquad\quad 12t = 12$
$\qquad\qquad t = 1$
Substitute $t = 1$ into Equation 3:
$2s = 7(1) - 15$
$2s = -8$
$\ s = -4$
So the solution of the system of linear
equations is $s = -4$ and $t = 1$.

16. $5x + 4y = -26$ — Equation 1
$5 - x = -6y$ — Equation 2
Use Equation 2 to solve for x in terms of y:
$5 - x = -6y$
$\qquad x = 6y + 5$ — Equation 3
Substitute Equation 3 into Equation 1:
$5(6y + 5) + 4y = -26$
$30y + 25 + 4y = -26$
$\qquad\qquad 34y = -51$
$$y = -\frac{3}{2}$$
Substitute $y = -\dfrac{3}{2}$ into Equation 3:
$$x = 6\left(-\frac{3}{2}\right) + 5$$
$\ \ = -4$
So the solution of the system of linear
equations is $x = -4$ and $y = -\dfrac{3}{2}$.

17. $3x + 5y = 35$ — Equation 1
$6x - 4y = -28$ — Equation 2
Multiply Equation 1 by 2:
$2(3x + 5y) = 2(35)$
$6x + 10y = 70$ — Equation 3
Subtract Equation 3 from Equation 2:
$(6x - 4y) - (6x + 10y) = -28 - 70$
$6x - 6x - 4y - 10y = -98$
$\qquad\qquad -14y = -98$
$\qquad\qquad\quad y = 7$

Substitute $y = 7$ into Equation 1:
$$3x + 5(7) = 35$$
$$3x + 35 = 35$$
$$x = 0$$
So the solution of the system of linear equations is $x = 0$ and $y = 7$.
Elimination method is used because substitution method will result in an algebraic fraction that will make the steps complicated.

18. $7m - 2n = -13$ — Equation 1
$2n - 5m = 11$ — Equation 2
Add Equation 1 and Equation 2:
$$(7m - 2n) + (2n - 5m) = -13 + 11$$
$$7m - 5m - 2n + 2n = -2$$
$$2m = -2$$
$$m = -1$$
Substitute $m = -1$ into Equation 1:
$$7(-1) - 2n = -13$$
$$-7 - 2n = -13$$
$$-2n = -6$$
$$n = 3$$
So the solution of the system of linear equations is $m = -1$ and $n = 3$.
Elimination method is used because substitution method will result in an algebraic fraction that will make the steps complicated.

19. $9m + 4n = 38$ — Equation 1
$2m = 5n - 21$ — Equation 2
Multiply Equation 1 by 2:
$$2(9m + 4n) = 2(38)$$
$$18m + 8n = 76$$ — Equation 3
Multiply Equation 2 by 9:
$$9(2m) = 9(5n - 21)$$
$$18m = 45n - 189$$ — Equation 4
Subtract Equation 4 from Equation 3:
$$(18m + 8n) - 18m = 76 - (45n - 189)$$
$$8n = 76 - 45n + 189$$
$$8n + 45n = 265$$
$$53n = 265$$
$$n = 5$$
Substitute $n = 5$ into Equation 1:
$$9m + 4(5) = 38$$
$$9m + 20 = 38$$
$$9m = 18$$
$$m = 2$$
So the solution of the system of linear equations is $m = 2$ and $n = 5$.
Elimination method is used because substitution method will result in an algebraic fraction that will make the steps complicated.

20. $5w - 4v = 1$ — Equation 1
$v = 6w + 14$ — Equation 2
Substitute Equation 2 into Equation 1:
$$5w - 4(6w + 14) = 1$$

$$5w - 24w - 56 = 1$$
$$-19w = 57$$
$$w = -3$$
Substitute $w = -3$ into Equation 2:
$$v = 6(-3) + 14$$
$$= -4$$
So the solution of the system of linear equations is $w = -3$ and $v = -4$.
Substitution method is used as v is already expressed in terms of w.

21. $2h + 9k = 19$ — Equation 1
$5h - 5k = 20$ — Equation 2
Multiply Equation 1 by 5:
$$5(2h + 9k) = 5(19)$$
$$10h + 45k = 95$$ — Equation 3
Multiply Equation 2 by 2:
$$2(5h - 5k) = 2(20)$$
$$10h - 10k = 40$$ — Equation 4
Subtract Equation 4 from Equation 3:
$$(10h + 45k) - (10h - 10k) = 95 - 40$$
$$10h - 10h + 45k + 10k = 55$$
$$55k = 55$$
$$k = 1$$
Substitute $k = 1$ into Equation 1:
$$2h + 9(1) = 19$$
$$2h + 9 = 19$$
$$2h = 10$$
$$h = 5$$
So the solution of the system of linear equations is $h = 5$ and $k = 1$.
Elimination method is used because substitution method will result in an algebraic fraction that will make the steps complicated.

22. $5y + 9 = 3x$ — Equation 1
$3x - 2y = 18$ — Equation 2
Substitute Equation 1 into Equation 2:
$$5y + 9 - 2y = 18$$
$$3y + 9 = 18$$
$$3y = 18 - 9$$
$$3y = 9$$
$$y = 3$$
Substitute $y = 3$ into Equation 1:
$$5(3) + 9 = 3x$$
$$3x = 24$$
$$x = 8$$
So the solution of the system of linear equations is $x = 8$ and $y = 3$.
Substitution method is used as $3x$ is already expressed in terms of y.

23. $3b + 4c = -6$ — Equation 1
$7b + 16c = -34$ — Equation 2
Multiply Equation 1 by 4:
$$4(3b + 4c) = 4(-6)$$
$$12b + 16c = -24$$ — Equation 3
Subtract Equation 3 from Equation 2:

$(7b + 16c) - (12b + 16c) = -34 - (-24)$
$7b - 12b + 16c - 16c = -34 + 24$
$$-5b = -10$$
$$b = 2$$
Substitute $b = 2$ into Equation 1:
$$3(2) + 4c = -6$$
$$6 + 4c = -6$$
$$4c = -6 - 6$$
$$4c = -12$$
$$c = -3$$
So the solution of the system of linear equations is $b = 2$ and $c = -3$.
Elimination method is used because substitution method will result in an algebraic fraction that will make the steps complicated.

24. $7p - q = 18$ — Equation 1
$3p + 4q = 21$ — Equation 2
Use Equation 1 to solve for q in terms of p:
$7p - q = 18$
$q = 7p - 18$ — Equation 3
Substitute Equation 3 into Equation 2:
$$3p + 4(7p - 18) = 21$$
$$3p + 28p - 72 = 21$$
$$31p = 21 + 72$$
$$31p = 93$$
$$p = 3$$
Substitute $p = 3$ into Equation 3:
$$q = 7(3) - 18$$
$$q = 3$$
So the solution of the system of linear equations is $p = 3$ and $q = 3$.
Substitution method is used as q can easily be expressed in terms of p.

Lesson 5.3

1. Let the number of art magazines be x and the number of science magazines be y.
$x + y = 26$ — Equation 1
$4x + 7y = 134$ — Equation 2
Solve Equation 1 for x in terms of y:
$x = 26 - y$ — Equation 3
Substitute Equation 3 into Equation 2:
$$4(26 - y) + 7y = 134$$
$$104 - 4y + 7y = 134$$
$$104 + 3y = 134$$
$$3y = 30$$
$$y = 10$$
Substitute $y = 10$ into Equation 3:
$$x = 26 - 10$$
$$x = 16$$

Jenny purchased 16 art magazines and 10 science magazines.

2. Let the number of adult tickets be x and the number of children's tickets be y.
$x + y = 95$ — Equation 1

$12x + 9y = 960$ — Equation 2
Solve Equation 1 for x in terms of y:
$x = 95 - y$ — Equation 3
Substitute Equation 3 into Equation 2:
$$12(95 - y) + 9y = 960$$
$$1,140 - 12y + 9y = 960$$
$$1,140 - 3y = 960$$
$$3y = 1,140 - 960$$
$$y = 60$$
Substitute $y = 60$ into Equation 3:
$x = 95 - 60$
$x = 35$
There were 35 adult tickets and 60 children's tickets sold.

3. Let the number of packets of roasted peanuts be x and the number of packets of beef jerky be y.
$5x + 3y = 37.80$ — Equation 1
$3x + 2y = 23.87$ — Equation 2
Multiply Equation 1 by 2:
$2(5x + 3y) = 2(37.80)$
$10x + 6y = 75.60$ — Equation 3
Multiply Equation 2 by 3:
$3(3x + 2y) = 3(23.87)$
$9x + 6y = 71.61$ — Equation 4
Subtract Equation 4 from Equation 3:
$(10x + 6y) - (9x + 6y) = 75.60 - 71.61$
$10x - 9x + 6y - 6y = 3.99$
$$x = 3.99$$
Substitute $x = 3.99$ into Equation 3:
$$10(3.99) + 6y = 75.60$$
$$39.90 + 6y = 75.60$$
$$6y = 35.70$$
$$y = 5.95$$
The cost of a packet of roasted peanuts is $3.99 and that of a packet of beef jerky is $5.95.

4. Let the number of wheat crackers a glass container can hold be x and the number of wheat crackers a plastic container can hold be y.
$6x + 2y = 180$ — Equation 1
$4x = 25 + 5y$ — Equation 2
Multiply Equation 1 by 2:
$2(6x + 2y) = 2(180)$
$12x + 4y = 360$ — Equation 3
Multiply Equation 2 by 3:
$3(4x) = 3(25 + 5y)$
$12x = 75 + 15y$ — Equation 4
Subtract Equation 4 from Equation 3:
$(12x + 4y) - 12x = 360 - (75 + 15y)$
$$4y = 360 - 75 - 15y$$
$$19y = 285$$
$$y = 15$$
Substitute $y = 15$ into Equation 3:

$12x + 4(15) = 360$
$12x + 60 = 360$
$12x = 300$
$x = 25$
Each glass container can hold 25 wheat crackers and each plastic container can hold 15 wheat crackers.

5. $10x - 7y = 36$ — Equation 1
$6x + 3y = 36$ — Equation 2
Divide Equation 2 by 3:
$6x + 3y = 36$
$2x + y = 12$ — Equation 3
Solve Equation 3 for y in terms of x:
$y = 12 - 2x$ — Equation 4
Substitute Equation 4 into Equation 1:
$10x - 7(12 - 2x) = 36$
$10x - 84 + 14x = 36$
$24x = 120$
$x = 5$
Substitute $x = 5$ into Equation 4:
$y = 12 - 2(5)$
$y = 12 - 10$
$= 2$
So the solution is $x = 5$ and $y = 2$.

6. a) $l = w + 3$ — Equation 1
$2(l + w) = 26$ — Equation 2
    b) Substitute Equation 1 into Equation 2:
$2(w + 3 + w) = 26$
$2(2w + 3) = 26$
$4w + 6 = 26$
$4w = 20$
$w = 5$
Substitute $w = 5$ into Equation 1:
$l = 5 + 3$
$= 8$
The length of the sandbox is 8 meters and the width of the sandbox is 5 meters.

7. Let the number of quarters be x and the number of dimes be y.
$10x + 25y = 1,675$ — Equation 1
$x + y = 85$ — Equation 2
Multiply Equation 2 by 10:
$10(x + y) = 10(85)$
$10x + 10y = 850$ — Equation 3
Subtract Equation 3 from Equation 1:
$(10x + 25y) - (10x + 10y) = 1,675 - 850$
$10x - 10x + 25y - 10y = 825$
$15y = 825$
$y = 55$
Substitute $y = 55$ into Equation 2:
$x + 55 = 85$
$x = 85 - 55$
$x = 30$
There are 30 quarters and 55 dimes in the vending machine.

8. Let the price of a card be x and the price of a photo frame be y.
$3x + 9y = 75$ — Equation 1
$8x + 5y = 67$ — Equation 2
Multiply Equation 1 by 8:
$8(3x + 9y) = 8(75)$
$24x + 72y = 600$ — Equation 3
Multiply Equation 2 by 3:
$3(8x + 5y) = 3(67)$
$24x + 15y = 201$ — Equation 4
Subtract Equation 4 from Equation 3:
$(24x + 72y) - (24x + 15y) = 600 - 201$
$24x - 24x + 72y - 15y = 399$
$57y = 399$
$y = 7$
Substitute $y = 7$ into Equation 2:
$8x + 5(7) = 67$
$8x + 35 = 67$
$8x = 32$
$x = 4$
The selling price of a card is \$4 and that of a photo frame is \$7.

9. a) Let the larger number be x and the smaller number be y.
$x + y = 31$ — Equation 1
$2x - 3y = 7$ — Equation 2
Multiply Equation 1 by 2:
$2(x + y) = 2(31)$
$2x + 2y = 62$ — Equation 3
Subtract Equation 3 from Equation 2:
$(2x - 3y) - (2x + 2y) = 7 - 62$
$2x - 2x - 3y - 2y = -55$
$-5y = -55$
$y = 11$
Substitute $y = 11$ into Equation 1:
$x + 11 = 31$
$x = 20$
The larger number is 20 and the smaller number is 11.

    b) Let the first number be x and the second number be y.
$x + 2y = 14$ — Equation 1
$x - y = 2$ — Equation 2
Subtract Equation 2 from Equation 1:
$(x + 2y) - (x - y) = 14 - 2$
$x - x + 2y + y = 12$
$3y = 12$
$y = 4$
Substitute $y = 4$ into Equation 2:
$x - 4 = 2$
$x = 6$
The first number is 6 and the second number is 4.

10. $35x + 20y = 310$ — Equation 1
$55x + 45y = 555$ — Equation 2

Multiply Equation 1 by 9:
$9(35x + 20y) = 9(310)$
$315x + 180y = 2,790$ — Equation 3
Multiply Equation 2 by 4:
$4(55x + 45y) = 4(555)$
$220x + 180y = 2,220$ — Equation 4
Subtract Equation 4 from Equation 3:
$(315x + 180y) - (220x + 180y) = 2,790 - 2,220$
$315x - 220x = 570$
$95x = 570$
$x = 6$
Substitute $x = 6$ into Equation 1:
$35(6) + 20y = 310$
$210 + 20y = 310$
$20y = 100$
$y = 5$
The entry fee for the seniors is $6 and that for the juniors is $5.

11. Let the number of pages in small font be x and that in large font be y.
$x + y = 12$ — Equation 1
$1,150x + 850y = 12,600$ — Equation 2
Solve Equation 1 for x in terms of y:
$x = 12 - y$ — Equation 3
Substitute Equation 3 into Equation 2:
$1,150(12 - y) + 850y = 12,600$
$13,800 - 1,150y + 850y = 12,600$
$-300y = -1200$
$y = 4$
Substitute $y = 4$ into Equation 3:
$x = 12 - 4$
$= 8$
8 pages in the document should be printed in small font and 4 pages should be printed in large font.

12. Let the number of gallons of 20% acidic solution be x and the number of gallons of 70% acidic solution be y.
$x + y = 24$ — Equation 1
20% of x + 70% of y = 50% of 24
$0.2x + 0.7y = 12$ — Equation 2
Solve Equation 1 for x in terms of y.
$x = 24 - y$ — Equation 3
Substitute Equation 3 into Equation 2:
$0.2(24 - y) + 0.7y = 12$
$4.8 - 0.2y + 0.7y = 12$
$0.5y = 7.2$
$y = 14.4$
Substitute $y = 14.4$ into Equation 3:
$x = 24 - 14.4$
$= 9.6$
Kelly should use 9.6 gallons of 20% acidic solution and 14.4 gallons of 70% acidic solution.

Lesson 5.4

1. a) $x - y = 1$

x	0	1	2
y	−1	0	1

$x + 2y = 4$

x	0	1	2
y	2	1.5	1

b)

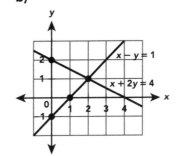

The point of intersection is (2, 1).

c) $x = 2$ and $y = 1$

2. a) $3x - 5y = 4$

x	−2	3	8
y	−2	1	4

$x + 2y = 5$

x	−1	1	5
y	3	2	0

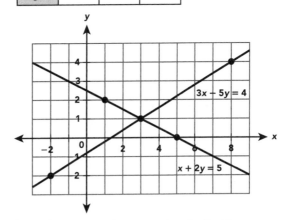

b) The point of intersection is (3, 1).

c) $x = 3$ and $y = 1$

3. a) $x - 3y = 5$

x	−1	2	5
y	−2	−1	0

$3x + 2y = 4$

x	0	2	4
y	2	−1	−4

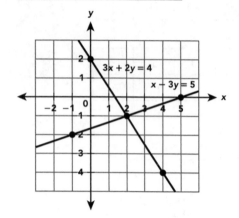

b) The point of intersection is (2, −1).

c) $x = 2$ and $y = −1$

4.

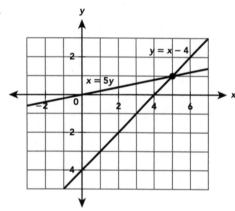

$x = 5, y = 1$

5.

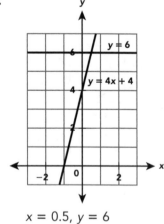

$x = 0.5, y = 6$

6.

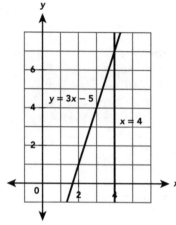

$x = 4, y = 7$

7.

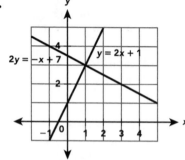

$x = 1, y = 3$

8.

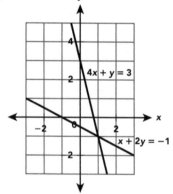

$x = 1, y = −1$

9.

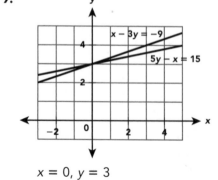

$x = 0, y = 3$

10. a) Note: In your graphing calculator, Y represents C.

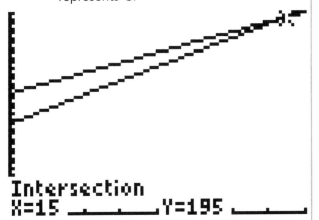

```
Intersection
X=15          Y=195
```

b) 15 campers

11. a) Note: In your graphing calculator, Y represents D.

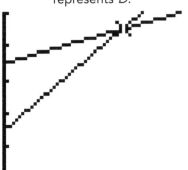

```
Intersection
X=2          Y=55
```

b) The two vehicles will meet 2 hours later.

12. a) Note: In your graphing calculator, Y represents L.

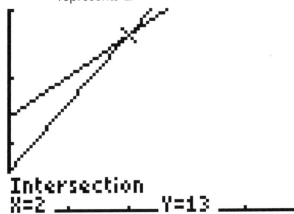

```
Intersection
X=2          Y=13
```

b) 2 pounds of weight attached to each spring will result in the springs stretching the same number of inches.

Lesson 5.5

1. $5x + 2y = 16$

x	0	2	3
y	8	3	0.5

$10x + 4y = 22$

x	1	2	3
y	3	0.5	−2

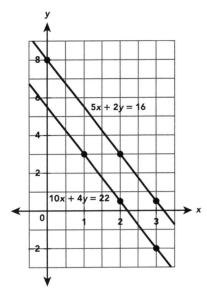

The system of linear equations is inconsistent.

2. $12x + 4y = 20$

x	0	1	2
y	5	2	−1

$3x + y = 5$

x	0	1	2
y	5	2	−1

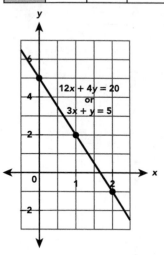

The system of linear equations is dependent.

3.

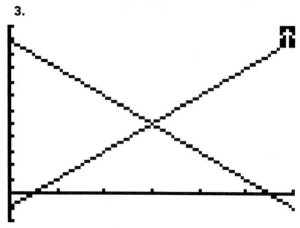

The system of linear equations is not dependent. It has a unique solution.

4.

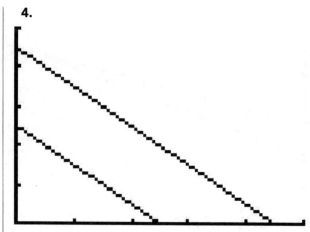

The system of linear equations is inconsistent.

5. $8x + 4y = 14$
$8x + 4y − 8x = 14 − 8x$
$\qquad 4y = 14 − 8x$
$\qquad y = 3.5 − 2x$

So the equation has slope −2 and y-intercept 3.5.
$2x + y = 28$
$2x + y − 2x = 28 − 2x$
$\qquad y = 28 − 2x$

So the equation has slope −2 and y-intercept 28.
When the two graphs have the same slope and different intercepts, they are parallel. The system of linear equations is inconsistent.

6. $12x − 3y = 9$
$12x − 3y − 12x = 9 − 12x$
$\qquad −3y = 9 − 12x$
$\qquad 3y = 12x − 9$
$\qquad y = 4x − 3$

So the equation has slope 4 and y-intercept −3.
$4x − y = 3$
$4x − y − 4x = 3 − 4x$
$\qquad −y = 3 − 4x$
$\qquad y = 4x − 3$

So the equation has slope 4 and y-intercept −3.
The two graphs represent the same line. The system of linear equations is dependent.

7. $-24x + 8y = 4$
$-24x + 8y - (-24x) = 4 - (-24x)$
$8y = 4 + 24x$
$y = 0.5 + 3x$

So the equation has slope 3 and y-intercept 0.5.

$-6x + 2y = 17$
$-6x + 2y - (-6x) = 17 - (-6x)$
$2y = 17 + 6x$
$y = 8.5 + 3x$

So the equation has slope 3 and y-intercept 8.5.

When the two graphs have the same slope and different intercepts, they are parallel. The system of linear equations is inconsistent.

8. $3x + 4y = 22$
$3x + 4y - 3x = 22 - 3x$
$4y = 22 - 3x$
$y = 5.5 - 0.75x$

So the equation has slope -0.75 and y-intercept 5.5.

$6x - 8y = 28$
$6x - 8y - 6x = 28 - 6x$
$-8y = 28 - 6x$
$y = 0.75x - 3.5$

So the equation has slope 0.75 and y-intercept -3.5.

The two graphs have different slopes and y-intercepts. The system of linear equations has a unique solution.

9. $4x + 9y = 7$
$4x + 9y - 4x = 7 - 4x$
$9y = 7 - 4x$
$y \quad \dfrac{7}{9} \quad \dfrac{4x}{9}$

So the equation has slope $-\dfrac{4}{9}$ and y-intercept $\dfrac{7}{9}$.

$16x + 36y = 28$
$16x + 36y - 16x = 28 - 16x$
$36y = 28 - 16x$
$y = \dfrac{7}{9} - \dfrac{4}{9}$

So the equation has slope $-\dfrac{4}{9}$ and y-intercept $\dfrac{7}{9}$.

The two graphs represent the same line. The system of linear equations is dependent.

10. $x + 5y = 17$
$x + 5y - x = 17 - x$
$5y = 17 - x$
$y = 3.4 - 0.2x$

So the equation has slope -0.2 and y-intercept 3.4.

$2x + 10y = 11$
$2x + 10y - 2x = 11 - 2x$
$10y = 11 - 2x$
$y = 1.1 - 0.2x$

So the equation has slope -0.2 and y-intercept 1.1.

When the two graphs have the same slope and different intercepts, they are parallel. The system of linear equations is inconsistent.

11. $12x + 36y = 54$
$12x + 36y - 12x = 54 - 12x$
$36y = 54 - 12x$
$y = 1.5 - \dfrac{1}{3}x$

So the equation has slope $-\dfrac{1}{3}$ and y-intercept 1.5.

$6x + 18y = 27$
$6x + 18y - 6x = 27 - 6x$
$18y = 27 - 6x$
$y = 1.5 - \dfrac{1}{3}x$

So the equation has slope $-\dfrac{1}{3}$ and y-intercept 1.5.

The two graphs represent the same line. The system of linear equations is dependent.

12. $2x + 3y = 5$
$2x + 3y - 2x = 5 - 2x$
$3y = 5 - 2x$
$y = \dfrac{5}{3} - \dfrac{2}{3}x$

So the equation has slope $-\dfrac{2}{3}$ and y-intercept $\dfrac{5}{3}$.

$14x + 21y = 35$
$14x + 21y - 14x = 35 - 14x$
$21y = 35 - 14x$
$y = \dfrac{5}{3} - \dfrac{2}{3}x$

So the equation has slope $-\dfrac{2}{3}$ and y-intercept $\dfrac{5}{3}$.

The two graphs represent the same line. The system of linear equations is dependent.

13. a) Let the cost of a one-night stay be n and the cost of one meal be m.
$2n + 3m = 185$ — Equation 1
$4n + 6m = 350$ — Equation 2

b)
$$2n + 3m = 185$$
$$2n + 3m - 2n = 184 - 2n$$
$$3m = 184 - 2n$$
$$m = \frac{184}{3} - \frac{2}{3}n$$
$$4n + 6m = 350$$
$$4n + 6m - 4n = 350 - 4n$$
$$6m = 350 - 4n$$
$$m = \frac{175}{3} - \frac{2}{3}n$$

The equations have the same slope and but different vertical intercepts. The system of linear equations is inconsistent.

c) The package Angela reserved to stay at the lodge has the least cost per day.

14. a) Let the length of plank B be x and the length of plank C be y.
Length of plank $A = 2x$
Length of plank $D = 2y$
$2x + 2y = 16$ — Equation 1
$x + y = 8$ — Equation 2

b)
$$2x + 2y - 2x = 16 - 2x$$
$$2y = 16 - 2x$$
$$y = 8 - x$$

So, the equation has slope -1 and y-intercept 8.
$$x + y - x = 8 - x$$
$$y = 8 - x$$

So, the equation has slope -1 and y-intercept 8.
The two equations represent the same line. The system of equations is dependent.

1. Let x be the tens place value of the number and y be the unit value of the number.
$x + y = 11$ — Equation 1
$10y + x - (10x + y) = 9$
$10y - y + x - 10x = 9$
$9y - 9x = 9$
$y - x = 1$ — Equation 2
Add Equation 1 and Equation 2:
$x + y + y - x = 11 + 1$
$2y = 12$
$y = 6$
Substitute $y = 6$ into Equation 1:
$x + 6 = 11$
$x = 5$
So the number is $50 + 6 = 56$.

2. $-4(x - 2) = 2 - 2x$
$-4x + 8 = 2 - 2x$
$-4x + 8 - 8 = 2 - 2x - 8$
$-4x = -2x - 6$
$-4x + 4x = -2x - 6 + 4x$
$2x - 6 = 0$
$2x = 6$
$x = 3$
$9 + 2(y - 3) - 3(y - 2) = 1$
$9 + 2y - 6 - 3y + 6 = 1$
$-y + 9 = 1$
$-y = -8$
$y = 8$

$$\frac{z}{3} + \frac{1}{2} = \frac{5}{2}$$
$$\frac{z}{3} + \frac{1}{2} - \frac{1}{2} = \frac{5}{2} - \frac{1}{2}$$
$$\frac{z}{3} = 2$$
$$z = 6$$

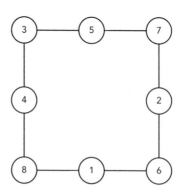

Chapter 6

Lesson 6.1

1. Input: Number of hours worked per week
   Output: Amount of weekly salary paid

2. Input: Time of the day
   Output: Length of shadow formed

3. Input: Gallons of gasoline
   Output: Distance travelled in miles

4. Many-to-many relation

5. One-to-one relation

6.

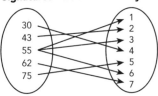

Many-to-one relation

7. **Number of Signatures**   **Relation**   **Day**

One-to-many relation

8. True. In a one-to-one relation there is exactly one output for each input.

9. True. A function is a special type of relation such that it pairs at most one output with every input.

10. True. Each icon when clicked on by Martha opens only one file.

11. False. It is not a function because there could be two pupils of the same age but of different heights.

12. One-to-many relation. No; because one input has more than one output, it is not a function.

13. One-to-one relation. Yes; because each input has exactly one output, it is a function.

14. Yes; because any vertical line only intersects the graph at exactly one point, it is a function.

15. Yes; because any vertical line only intersects the graph at exactly one point, it is a function.

16. No; because there is one vertical line that intersects the graph at two points, it is not a function.

17. Yes; because any vertical line only intersects the graph at exactly one point, it is a function.

18.

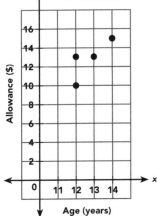

19.

Savings

20. a)

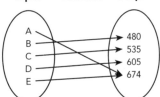

   b) Many-to-one relation

   c) Yes; it is a function because each input produces exactly one output.

21. a) **Input**   **Relation**   **Output**

   b) Many-to-one relation. Yes; it is a function because each input produces exactly one output.

c)

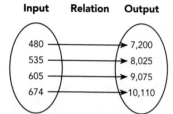

Input	Relation	Output
480	→	7,200
535	→	8,025
605	→	9,075
674	→	10,110

One-to-one relation. Yes, it is a function because each input produces exactly one output.

Lesson 6.2

1. The total number of words typed equals the product of 75 and the number of minutes.
$N = 75t$

2. The total amount paid equals the sum of the flat fee plus 10 times the number of days.
$y = 50 + 10d$

3.

x	10	11	12
y	120	132	144

$y = 12x$

4. $A = 72 - 5t$

t	1	2	3
A	67	62	57

5. $y = -2$

6. $y = \frac{2}{5}x + 2$

7.

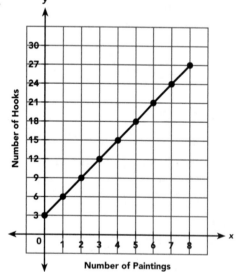

8. $y = 35 + 70x$

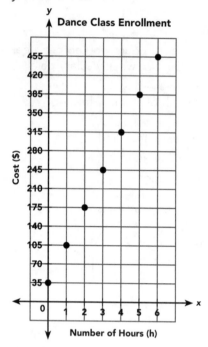

9. a) $y = 360 - 90x$

   b) The slope, -90, represents the rate at which the sheets of paper are used. The number of sheets of paper in the input tray decreases by 90 sheets per minute.

10. a) The amount of money on the card equals 45 minus the product of 7.5 and the number of movies watched, x. The algebraic equation is $y = 45 - 7.5x$

   b)

x	0	1	2	3	4	5	6
y	45.0	37.5	30.0	22.5	15.0	7.50	0

   c)

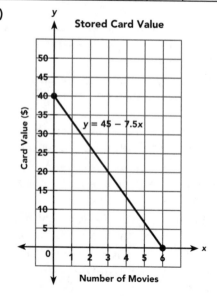

Lesson 6.3

1. Nonlinear function
2. Linear function
3. Linear function
4. Nonlinear function
5. No
6. Yes; Rate of change = −1
7. Linear and increasing function
8. Nonlinear and decreasing function
9. Nonlinear and increasing function
10. Linear and decreasing function
11. **a)** Least possible input is 0 (when no one presses on the dispense button) and the corresponding output value is 3,300 milliliters. As the number of presses on the dispense button increases, the volume of beverage in the dispensing machine decreases. Because each press dispenses a constant volume of hot beverage, the rate of change of the function is constant. So the function is a decreasing linear function.

b) V (ml)

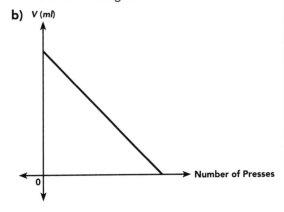

12. **a)** At 0 speed, no data is downloaded. So, the least possible input value is 0 and the corresponding output value is 0. As the speed increases, the amount of data downloaded also increases. Because the speed of downloading is not constant, the function is an increasing nonlinear function.

b) D

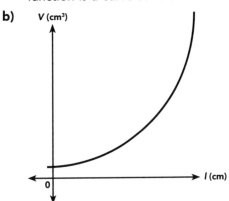

13. **a)** The rate of change is not constant. The function is a curve so it is nonlinear.

b) V (cm³)

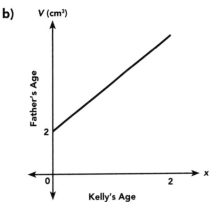

Every point on the graph is an input of the side length of the cube and its corresponding output of volume.

14. **a)** The function is an increasing linear function.

b) V (cm³)

Every point on the graph is an input of Kelly's age and the corresponding output of her father's age.

Lesson 6.4

1. No
2. Yes
3. No
4. Yes
5. No
6. Yes
7. No
8. Yes
9. No
10. Yes

11. a) Both functions are increasing linear functions. The function for Tank A has a greater rate of change than the function for Tank B.

b)

Tank A: $V = 80 + 25t$

Time (t minutes)	0	1	2	3	4	5	6
Volume of Water (V liters)	80	105	130	155	180	205	230

Tank B: $V = 100 + 15t$

Time (t minutes)	0	1	2	3	4	5	6
Volume of Water (V liters)	100	115	130	145	160	175	190

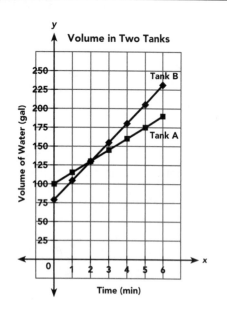

c) The graph shows that after 2 minutes, tank A is being filled up at a faster rate than tank B. So tank A will fill up first.

12. a) Option A: $y = 10t + 25$ and Option B: $y = 12t + 20$

b) Both functions are increasing linear functions. Comparing the two equations, $25 > 20$, option A has a higher basic rate at first. Comparing the rate of change, Option A charges $10 for hourly labor, and Option B charges $12 for hourly labor. So the amount Option B charges will increase more rapidly than the amount Option A charges.

13. a) $y = 9{,}000 - 90t$

b) Machine B. It can churn 5,000 pounds of butter in less time.

Brain@Work

1. a) $C = 500 + 2 \cdot p$
$C = 2p + 500$

b)

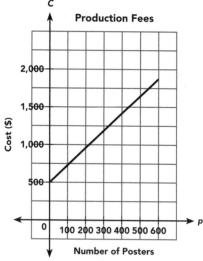

c) $P = 4p - (2p + 500)$
$P = 4p - 2p - 500$
$P = 2p - 500$

d)

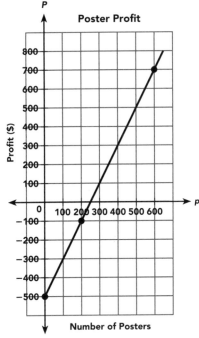

Poster Profit

e) From the graph, 250 posters must be sold to break even.

Cumulative Practice for Chapters 5 to 6

1. $4x + 3y = 13$

x	1	3	4
y	3	$\frac{1}{3}$	-1

$2x - 7y = 15$

x	1	3	4
y	$-\frac{13}{7}$	$-\frac{9}{7}$	-1

Only the pair of values $x = 4$ and $y = -1$ appear in both tables. So the solution of the system of equations is $x = 4$ and $y = -1$.

2. $y - 4x = 16$

x	-2	0	2
y	8	16	24

$6y + x = 46$

x	-2	0	2
y	8	$\frac{23}{3}$	$\frac{22}{3}$

Only the pair of values $x = -2$ and $y = 8$ appear in both tables. So the solution of the system of equations is $x = -2$ and $y = 8$.

3. $x - y + 5 = 0$ — Eq. 1
$x + 4y = 25$ — Eq. 2
Subtract Equation 2 from Eq.1:
$(x - y + 5) - (x + 4y) = 0 - 25$
$x - y + 5 - x - 4y = -25$
$-5y + 5 - 5 = -25 - 5$
$-5y = -30$
$y = 6$
Substitute $y = 6$ into Equation1:
$x - 6 + 5 = 0$
$x - 1 = 0$
$x = 1$
So the solution of the system of linear equations is $x = 1$ and $y = 6$.
Elimination method is used as it is easier.

4. $6x + 4y = 64$ — Eq. 1
$2x + 3y = 23$ — Eq. 2
Multiply Eq. 2 by 3:
$3(2x + 3y) = 3(23)$
$6x + 9y = 69$ — Eq. 3
Subtract Eq. 3 from Eq.1:
$(6x + 4y) - (6x + 9y) = 64 - 69$
$6x - 6x + 4y - 9y = -5$
$-5y = -5$
$y = 1$
Substitute $y = 1$ into Eq.1:
$6x + 4(1) = 64$
$6x + 4 = 64$
$6x + 4 - 4 = 64 - 4$
$6x = 60$
$x = 10$
So the solution of the system of linear equations is $x = 10$ and $y = 1$. Elimination method is used as substitution method will result in an algebraic fraction that will make the steps complicated.

5. $\frac{1}{2}x + y = 1$ — Eq. 1

$\frac{1}{4}x - 2y = 8$ — Eq. 2

Use Eq. 1 to solve for y in terms of x:

$\frac{1}{2}x + y = 1$

$y = 1 - \frac{1}{2}x$ — Eq. 3

Substitute Eq. 3 into Eq. 2:

$\frac{1}{4}x - 2\left(1 - \frac{1}{2x}\right) = 8$

$\frac{1}{4}x - 2 + x = 8$

$\frac{5}{4}x - 2 + 2 = 8 + 2$

$\frac{5}{4}x = 10$

$x = 8$

Substitute $x = 8$ into Eq. 3:
$$y = 1 - \frac{1}{2}(8)$$
$$= 1 - 4$$
$$= -3$$
So the solution of the system of linear equations is $x = 8$ and $y = -3$.
Substitution method is used as y can be easily expressed in terms of x.

6. $4x - y = -3$ — Eq. 1
$x + y = 8$ — Eq. 2
Add Eq. 1 and Eq. 2:
$(4x - y) + (x + y) = -3 + 8$
$4x - y + x + y = 5$
$5x = 5$
$x = 1$
Substitute $x = 1$ into Eq. 2:
$1 + y = 8$
$y = 7$
So the solution of the system of linear equations is $x = 1$ and $y = 7$.
Elimination method is used as it is easier.

7.

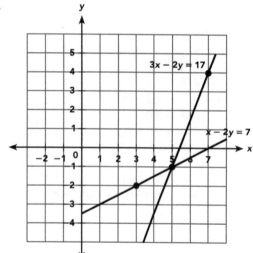

8.

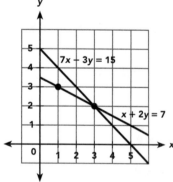

9. $x + 2y = 5$ — Eq. 1
$2x + 4y = 10$ — Eq. 2
Rewrite the equations in slope-intercept form $y = ax + b$.
Eq. 1

$x + 2y = 5$
$x + 2y - x = 5 - x$
$2y = 5 - x$
$y = \frac{5}{2} - \frac{1}{2}x$

Eq. 2
$2x + 4y = 10$
$x + 2y = 5$
$x + 2y - x = 5 - x$
$2y = 5 - x$
$y = \frac{5}{2} - \frac{1}{2}x$

The equations are the same. So, this system of linear equations has an infinite number of solutions. Therefore, it is dependent.

10. $\frac{2}{3}x - y = 1$ — Eq. 1

$2x - 3y = 7$ — Eq. 2
Rewrite the equations in slope-intercept form $y = ax + b$.
Eq. 1

$\frac{2}{3}x - y = 1$

$\frac{2}{3}x - y - \frac{2}{3}x = 1 - \frac{2}{3}x$

$-y = 1 - \frac{2}{3}x$

$y = \frac{2}{3}x - 1$

Eq. 2
$2x - 3y = 7$
$2x - 3y - 2x = 7 - 2x$
$-3y = 7 - 2x$
$y = \frac{2}{3}x - \frac{7}{3}$

The equations have the same slope and different y-intercepts. The system of linear equations is inconsistent.

11. $\frac{1}{3}x - 3y = 1$ — Eq. 1
$x = 9y + 8$ — Eq. 2
Rewrite the equations in slope-intercept form $y = ax + b$.
Eq. 1

$\frac{1}{3}x - 3y = 1$

$\frac{1}{3}x - 3y - \frac{1}{3}x = 1 - \frac{1}{3}x$

$-3y = 1 - \frac{1}{3}x$

$y = \frac{1}{9}x - \frac{1}{3}$

Eq. 2
$x = 9y + 8$
$9y + 8 = x$
$9y + 8 - 8 = x - 8$

$$9y = x - 8$$
$$y = \frac{1}{9}x - \frac{8}{9}$$

The equations have the same slope and different y-intercepts. The system of linear equations is inconsistent.

12. $7x - 14y - 28 = 0$ — Eq. 1
$3x = 12 - 6y$ — Eq. 2
Rewrite the equations in slope-intercept form $y = ax + b$.
Eq. 1
$7x - 14y - 28 = 0$
$14y - 7x + 28 = 0$
$14y - 7x + 28 + 7x - 28 = 0 + 7x - 28$
$14y = 7x - 28$
$y = \frac{1}{2}x - 2$
Eq. 2
$$3x = 12 - 6y$$
$$12 - 6y = 3x$$
$$12 - 6y - 12 = 3x - 12$$
$$-6y = 3x - 12$$
$$y = \frac{1}{2}x - 2$$

The equations are the same. So, this system of linear equations has an infinite number of solutions. Therefore, it is dependent.

13. Yes; Because each input has exactly one output, it is a function.

14. Yes; Because each input has exactly one output, it is a function.

15. No; Because one input, -2, has more than 1 output, it is not a function.

16. Yes; Because each input has exactly one output, it is a function.

17. $x = 75t$

18. $y = 8 + 2x$

19.

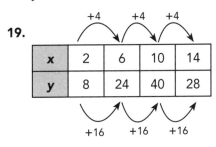

x	2	6	10	14
y	8	24	40	28

Rate of change $= \frac{16}{4} = 4$
Because the rate of change is constant, the table represents a linear function. It is an increasing function.

20. The function is non linear and increasing.

21.

Questions Answered Correctly	Relation	Total Score
1	→	3
2	→	6
3	→	9
4	→	12
5	→	15

It is a function. Each input has exactly one output.

22. Let the age of Mr. Nelson be x and the age of his son, John be y.
$x = 9y$ — Eq. 1
$x + 9 = 3(y + 9)$
$x + 9 = 3y + 27$
$x = 3y + 18$ — Eq. 2
Substitute Eq. 1 into Eq. 2:
$9y = 3y + 18$
$9y - 3y = 3y + 18 - 3y$
$6y = 18$
$y = 3$
Substitute $y = 3$ into Eq. 1:
$x = 9(3)$
$\quad = 27$
Mr. Nelson is 27 years old now and his son, John is 3 years old now.

23. a)
$$3x + 11 = x + 7y$$
$$3x - x - 11 + 11 = x + 7y - x - 11$$
$$2x = 7y - 11 \quad \text{— Eq. 1}$$
$$x + 7y = 2(3y + 4)$$
$$x + 7y = 6y + 8$$
$$x + 7y - 6y = 6y + 8 - 6y$$
$$x + y = 8 \quad \text{— Eq. 2}$$
Use Eq. 2 to solve for x in terms of y:
$$x = 8 - y \quad \text{— Eq. 3}$$
Substitute Eq. 3 into Eq. 1:
$$2x = 7y - 11$$
$$2(8 - y) = 7y - 11$$
$$16 - 2y = 7y - 11$$
$$16 - 2y + 11 + 2y = 7y - 11 + 11 + 2y$$
$$27 = 9y$$
$$y = 3$$
Substitute $y = 3$ into Eq. 3:
$$x = 8 - 3$$
$$\quad = 5$$

b) $3(5) + 11 = 26$
The length of each side of the regular hexagon is 26 inches.

24. a) $C = 30 + 10n$

b)

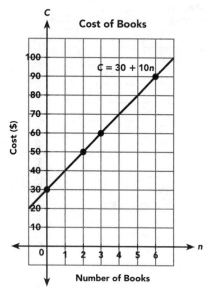

Cost of Books

c) The y-intercept, 30, means that Priscilla pays $30 first before joining the book club. The slope, 10, gives the rate at which the cost of book is changing. For every book that Priscilla buys, the total amount she pays increases by $10.

25. Let 1 lb of ham cost $x and 1 lb of turkey cost $y.

$2x + 3y = 92$ — Eq. 1
$5x + 2y = 120$ — Eq. 2
Multiply Eq. 1 by 5:
$5(2x + 3y) = 5(92)$
$10x + 15y = 460$ — Eq. 3
Multiply Eq. 2 by 2:
$2(5x + 2y) = 2(120)$
$10x + 4y = 240$ — Eq. 4
Subtract Eq. 4 from Eq. 3:
$(10x + 15y) - (10x + 4y) = 460 - 240$
$10x + 15y - 10x - 4y = 220$
$11y = 220$
$y = 20$

26. a) $A = 5 - 0.25n$

b) If Kenny does not buy any toy capsules, he spends $0. So, the least possible input value is 0 and the corresponding output value is $5. As Kenny buys more toy capsules, the amount of money he has left decreases. Since each toy capsule cost the same, the rate of change of the function is constant. So the function is a decreasing linear function.

c)

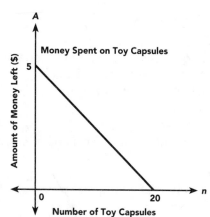

Money Spent on Toy Capsules

27. a) $x + y = 180$ — Eq. 1
$y = 4x$ — Eq. 2

b)

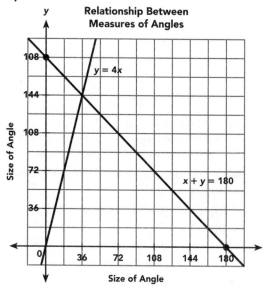

Relationship Between Measures of Angles

c) The size of the angles will never be the same.